Closer To Truth

Closer To Love

The Mystic Chronicles

Present

Closer To Truth
Closer To Love

A Spiritual Guide To

Inner Peace And Empowerment

By

Black Warrior

Closer To Truth-Closer To Love
A Spiritual Guide to Inner Peace and Empowerment

Copyright © 2013 Black Warrior

Cover Design by: Aquil Johnston

Published by: Mystic Fire Publications

Editors: Black Warrior
        Alison Guerin-Cameron

Photography: Ricardo Johnston Jr.
               Kimshala Hibbert

ISBN: 978-0-9910661-0-0 (paperback)

Website Design by: Aquil Johnston

Websites: http://www.closertotruthclosertolove.com
       : http://www.blackwarriorbook.com
       : http://www.blackwarriormusic.com

Contents

Contents

Contents

Contents

Words Of Light

For *humanity to truly attain Freedom of mind, body and spirit; and allow Peace to flourish abundantly within: To the point that it becomes our normality and our reality. We the Children of God and this great Universe must embrace the highest and simplest Wisdom: Wisdom that elevates us to a realm of Righteousness: Wisdom that mandates that **Truth** will now and forever be harmoniously united with **Love**. For without truth love is nothing but an illusion. Without truth love becomes unhealthy, tainted and impure. Without truth love loses its identity. For where there's no love, there can never be Peace... For that too shall remain an illusion!*

Closer To Truth
        Closer To Love
                Black Warrior

You Are My Friend

If you need someone who understands and feels the depths of your pain then I'm your friend. If you long to embrace someone who for their entire life has been free of selfishness, greed and malice then I'm your friend. If hopelessness and despair have brought you to your knees and you need to be lifted high above the heavens then I'm your friend. If you're sick and tired of the lies and are ready for truth then I'm your friend. If you're in search of someone who has faithfully sacrificed their material comforts so that they can be an Inspired Warrior for healing and enlightenment then I am your friend. And if what you yearn for is a life rich with love, truth and empowerment then I am and forever will be, Your Very Best Friend!

Closer To Truth
Closer To Love
Black Warrior

Recommendations

(The Welcome Mat)

Greetings everyone! Welcome to my presentation of Closer to Truth Closer to Love: (A Spiritual Guide to Inner Peace and Empowerment). First I want to thank you for deciding to explore my work. This journey you are about to embark on is designed to take you higher spiritually. It is designed to open up your mind and gradually feed you important information. Information, that would not only help to pinpoint the root causes of toxicities you're more likely to be plagued with; But more importantly enlighten you to the solutions. This book is structured in such a way that simplifies it and minimizes the shock value of its forthcoming content. It is for precisely this reason I strongly recommend that the chapters be read chronologically. To not do so, is likely to create some unnecessary conflict and confusion. It would be similar to taking the main course of a subject before taking the prerequisite; Or rendering a just verdict before all the evidence have been presented... If you take my advice, I am confident that what you're about to discover will have a much more positive and greater impact. Which will enable you to enjoy the full benefit of our journey (this book).

I've also included an impromptu treat I came up with while writing one of the chapters. I've purposely chosen not to list it in order to create some mystique and excitement. So again, I urge you to play fair and not go looking for it. Hopefully when you do come upon it, you'll enjoy reading it as much as I've enjoyed writing it. So relax, take a deep breath and have fun!

Acknowledgments

To The Most High Creator of all things, whose spirit abides within me and through whom everything is possible including this book. I give all Thanks and the Highest Praise...

To the Ancestors and the Ancestral Warriors whose shoulders I firmly stand on, I give all Thanks and Praise.

To my father Samuel "The Lord" Johnston, I thank you in every way. You motivate me like no other. Without you this book would have only been an idea. When I first pitched it to you, you seemed to have instantly known the fullness of its importance. You saw the vision, and you consistently got on me until I got it done. Therefore I dedicate this book to you. You have proven to not only be the greatest father, but also the greatest friend...

What can I say about you Mom? You're the Queen

and I love you more than life itself. Because of you I'm unquestionably the most blessed man in the world. You consistently support me and everyone else without ever making us feel like we're being a burden. Honestly, I don't know how you do it. You are more than amazing! Your love is truly priceless...

To my brother and riding partner Reds aka Marlon, the man who fears nothing and could do any and everything. Listen man, you've proven how much you believe not only in this book but also me, by taking on the responsibility of getting the world to hear my message. With the power that you possess, I know it will get done. So Thank You! And I also want to thank in advance the team you're putting together. I know it's going to be awesome.

Special thanks and appreciation go out to Alison Guerin–Cameron. Your constructive criticisms and priceless assistance in helping to edit this book has enabled me to bring it that much closer to perfection. All Love and Blessings to you and your entire family...

To my beautiful children all of whom I love more that life itself. I want to thank you all for helping out with this book. Hopefully none of you will make me out to be a liar. Ok! India, Ricky, Ian, Nigel, and Aquil! I have faith in you guys, I know you're going to come through and make use of the extraordinary talents you've all been blessed with. Honestly, I'm amazed by *how great you guys are, and more importantly, how much greater you can become. This world is truly yours!!!*

To my beautiful grandchildren, grandpa loves you all more than anything. You are living proof of my existence. May all your lives be eternally filled with Blessings and consumed with Love... Oh! Just in case anyone is wondering about my age, I started extremely young, like 13. So cut it out with the old man jokes...

To everyone in my extremely large family that includes: All my brothers and sisters, my aunts and uncles, my cousins, my nieces and nephews, and all their partners, Maximum Love and Blessings to you all...

Hey Nicole hang in their baby; you're much stronger than you know. Your adversity woke up the sleeping giant in you. I can see it...

What's up Shawn the conquering Lion? In you I see victory, I truly believe there's nothing you can't conquer. It's all up to you, you were born to win and you will...

Hey Wendel, the man called Heads; in you I see brilliance. I've got so much respect for you it's unbelievable. You're probably the most organically talented person I know. You inspire me!

Acknowledgments

What's up Midge, little brother? What they call you Bryan, or Richard? Whatever! Listen! Anyone who underestimates you is making a huge mistake. You got power and talent. Maybe it's time to show the world what you've got.

Hey Portia! Lil sister, you used to be such a badass. Remember when you used to whip peoples behind, including the guys. They couldn't believe how someone so pretty could be so tough. I think you're a gifted person. Its time to use your power, just don't punch anyone...

What's up Barry, Mr. Cool? You're so cool you remind me of myself. At least how I used to be. These days I tend to make a little more noise. I wish we had spent more time together. Hopefully that would change in the near future. Listen man, All Love and Blessings to you and the rest of your family.

Hey Dexter, I know you thought I forgot about you. I would never do that. You're my brother in every sense of the word. You are one of the most selfless people I know. You are more than a Blessing. All Love and Blessings to you and your family...

Hey! What's up Uncle Courtney? Oh! Excuse me Cutney. You are without question the bridge of the family. You always make it your duty to connect with everyone. I want to thank you for your love and support. All Love and Blessings to you and your entire crew.

I've got to mention the old genius. What's up uncle Hector? It appears to me you're one of those who may make it to the century. I sincerely hope you do. All Love and Blessings to you and your entire posse.

To all my friends too numerous to mention, you know who you are. All Love and Blessings to you and your families.

I've got to acknowledge some spiritually gifted and enlightened friends who were pivotal in my spiritual growth. Friends like Queen Ella Andall, Delores De La Paz, and Christine Lewis to name some. All Love and Blessings to you and your entire families. Thank you for the friendship and for loving me the way you have.

Special thanks and appreciation go out to some personal friends whose technical advice and support has made it much easier for me to do what I've been doing musically and otherwise. Friends like Pierre Salandy and Tony Benjamin. Hey guys, your friendship and assistance have been priceless. All Love and Blessings to you and your entire families.

Big up to the great Ziggy Marley for doing the song "Love Is My Religion". Obviously a lot of people didn't fully get it, hopefully that will soon change. I want you to know the spirit of your father is definitely an important part of my existence and I feel a deep connection to him. I dedicate the Chapter "Love Is My Religion" to you, your father, your mother and your entire family. Maximum Love and Blessings to every one of you.

To all those lovely ladies who've brought both sunshine and rain into my life, I sincerely thank you for both. We all need a little sunshine and rain in order for us to grow. It was never my intention to hurt anyone of you. But we've all got to be true to ourselves. Why would we want to be any other way? I want you all to know I have nothing but love and appreciation for each and every one of you, no exceptions and no regrets. I wish you all the best life has to offer...

Finally to all my readers, I want every one of you to know that I'm extremely grateful you've decided to take this journey with me, allowing me to enter into your hearts and minds. My heart is filled with appreciation. I am truly privileged! Maximum Love and Blessings to each and every one of you and your families.

I hope everyone not only enjoys this book, but also benefits from it...

Introduction

(The Why)

*W*hy am I writing this book you might ask? The why that's why. Exactly! Confused are you? Don't be! As a child growing up on the island of Trinidad, I always had the need to know (the why) of things. Particularly the things that appeared negative and troubling to me. I was extremely observant and possessed a very high level of curiosity. As I grew older my desire to know grew even stronger. Not only to have a deeper understanding of those "whys", but more importantly to find the solutions to the more problematic ones.

This book is a comprehensive exposé of those troubling whys, and my recommended solutions to the problems they've been inflicting on humanity. It is about the solutions that have manifested in me as a result of my spiritual growth. This book is an unveiling of the wisdom and vision that was born through my relationship with the power that abides within me. And that power is my **Inner God**...

This book is about doing what I truly believe I was

*born to do. Which is to passionately do all I can to inspire the transformation of planet earth into a united and peaceful world. A feat I fully intend to see fulfilled during my lifetime and not somewhere in the distant future. This book is about **Truth**, the truth through my spiritual eye.*

"Without truth there's no reality, all that exists is fantasy. Without truth, there is no freedom, and without freedom there is no justice and no peace".

*Now before we go any further, I want to clarify my use of the term **God** in the context of being "The Supreme Being". So when I use the term God in this context, I'm referring to the **Creator** of the Universe; He, she, it, or maybe even them. In other words, whomever or whatever gave birth to this great Universe is what I'm referring to as **God**, or **The Creator**. With that, let's get back to truth.*

(Truth)

What is truth? Truth is power. Truth is honesty. Truth is liberation. Truth is, what is or what was in its exactness without deviation. Truth makes perfection possible. The more we embrace truth the closer to perfection we become. Truth brings us closer to God and God is perfection. It is precisely for this reason we as a people need to conform to the

**truth and not the other way around, as we have been
consistently doing with chronic recklessness.**

*Sadly... Truth has become irrelevant in today's
society. It seems that people are more obsessed with
being politically correct or maintaining their personal
and emotional agendas than being truthful. One has to
be extremely careful of what they say these days. It
seems the more truthful you are, the more liable you
are to have some power hungry mogul or enraged
fanatic threatening your life or your livelihood. We
have become so corrupted and dysfunctional that the
truth is often seen as a threat. It is the prime reason
our society has been so misguided and troubled.
According to a line in a powerful song titled **"Shame"**,
by an equally powerful friend of mine (Queen Ella
Andall of Trinidad & Tobago) who says: **"Truth has
taken a name change"**. She is absolutely correct. The
truth simply isn't the truth anymore and it hasn't been
for a very long time.*

*The problem is; there are too many people in high
places that are way too deep into their untruths to
admit it. In many instances their entire existence is
built on them upholding and perpetuating these lies.
Then there are others who are just too embarrassed or
afraid to admit they have been misled. They know if
they do, they're likely to be discredited. **Unless we
embrace truth with unwavering urgency, there's no
way we could survive.** Our world is now at its*

crossroads. We're in the midst of an extremely crucial transitionary period the likes of which we've never seen before. This cannot be overstated. Our untruths have finally caught up with us. Our flawed cannibalistic system (as I choose to call it) along with our reckless disregard for nature and the atmosphere is disrupting any hopes of humanity attaining a harmonious, peaceful and healthy world. To borrow a boxing term, humanity's existence is on the ropes receiving an eight count, literally on the verge of a devastating collapse, and greed is definitely the culprit. If we don't do something to significantly alter the situation we could all be doomed.

Why are so many of us suffering? How have we allowed ourselves to become so unhealthy? It seems insanity has become the norm. Toxicity levels are way too high. We have simply lost our soul and our conscience. The majority of people are becoming poorer and poorer, while a minute amount is steadily becoming richer and richer. It feels as though hoards of money are being shipped to Mars or Jupiter. The truth is, capitalism is a very sophisticated form of slavery. It has gotten so bad that some nations are economically collapsing. It's only a matter of time before the 99% rise up to completely overthrow the insanely wealthy 1%. Not only here in America but all across the globe. We've recently had a very serious scare but the next time we won't be so lucky. This vicious and blatant unfairness has to stop. If not, it will serve to unite the oppressed 99% with unrelenting impartiality. Watch out!

We are also seeing current efforts to minimize the amount of Americans being killed by gun violence blocked as a result of greed. Americans are killing themselves and each other at a level higher than any of their foreign wars combined. It makes me wonder about our humanity. Where's the love my people??? Where's the love we all need to survive? We are clearly in dire need of it as our children continuously cry out in pain. Can't you hear them? **"If you close your eyes and look within, then you will clearly see and know that we are desperately in need of love and truth".**

(Lifestyles)

Our social behavior is in shambles. The lifespan of romantic relationships are increasingly growing shorter and shorter. The marriage institution is in a very dilapidated state. It seems to be doing more harm than good. The conventional family structure is rapidly becoming a thing of the past, particularly within the African American community where 72% of children are being raised in a single parent household. It is absolutely indisputable that what we've been doing thus far as a whole is clearly not working. For us to continue on in this same direction would be pure and unmitigated insanity. I don't mean to be negative, but if we intend to heal our world and ourselves, we need to discover why so many things keep falling apart. We really don't have much choice. We must get to the root and truth of the matter. It is the only way we can implement the correct changes and begin the healing process; with complete and total honesty.

(Genesis)

Just to give you a brief history of my beginnings. I was born on the twin island of Trinidad, with the sister island being Tobago. I am the eldest of eight children: Four brothers and two sisters from both parents, with one additional brother from my father.

According to my parents (who by the way are still alive and together), I was the perfect child. I was obedient, highly intelligent and very peaceful. I had a mystical way about me. According to them I was clearly special. Many of their friends would often challenge me at spelling words whenever they came by. Big mistake!!! The words were sometimes a little difficult but I always seem to get them right. Words like Mississippi just to name one.

They said I would lift my head to the heavens and correctly spell the words. At the time I was just about two years old.

Introduction

My parents' friends were so amazed by my ability to spell those words at such an early age; they would give me money for it. It is how I was able to fill my piggy bank.

This trend started, when a friend of my father by the name of Peter asked me to spell certain words for him. When I did, he was so impressed he gave me five dollars. Back in those days five dollars was a weekly salary to many Trinidadians.

*My childhood was extremely rich with love and happiness, and though we lived in a one-bedroom home, my siblings and I were all comfortable. We always had enough to eat and always looked fashionable. Both our parents sewed professionally. My father was a tailor and my mother a seamstress. So clothing was never an issue. There was so much happiness permeating the air it was unavoidable. Laughter and excitement was everywhere. **It was very clear and obvious that I came into this world with unquestionable love, and not sin**.*

(My Parents)

What can I say about my parents? They are simply the greatest. My mother is the manifestation of true beauty; She was and still is the platinum standard. She is trusted and respected by everyone who knows her. She is the most loving, caring, hardworking and generous person you could ever know. She is without question the embodiment of motherhood. She only has one tiny obsession (if you could call it that). She has a fixation with being in shape. Especially for herself and her family. So she goes to the gym three times a week. At age 75 after having seven children, her stomach is still flat. So you don't have any excuses. She would say "I see you're getting a little chubby around the stomach there what's going on?" And you can't even hide it because she has eyes like a hawk. Oh! I almost forgot! She's also a basketball fanatic. Warning! You can't say anything bad about Lebron James; if you do you're going to get smacked. I'm not kidding; she might even kick you, out of her house that is. Well! Maybe I'm exaggerating just a bit, but my advice to you is to keep your mouth shut. Other than that, she is an angel.

My father is simply the greatest man. He is great at almost everything he does. He is the fairest and most generous person I know. I remember him taking a few ice cream bars and sharing it among all the children in the yard, and there were a lot of us. His belief was everyone had to get a piece. He would give you his last dollar if he thought you needed it more than he did. He had zero tolerance for bullies and advantageous people. All fools who crossed that line in his presence met their quick demise. He would whoop that behind in record time. He was a great athlete and track star. Had it not been for injury, he probably would have been in the Olympics. He is also a great musician, songwriter and singer. At age 78 he's built like a ninja warrior. Everyone who knows him including some of the guys whose behinds he had whooped, love him. He is so good, that his peers named him 'The Lord' way back in the 1960's. I'm not kidding. Due to his ability to see things before they happened, combined with his sheer power and greatness as a man, that's what they called him. That name has stuck to him ever since. That's what I call him today, The Lord.

(Culture & Spirituality)

The yard I grew up in was a cultural and spiritual powerhouse. Along with my parents' home, my grandmother and two of my uncles also lived in separate homes in the same yard.

Culturally! *My uncle is one of the greatest pioneers of the steel drum instrument, if not THE greatest that ever walked the planet earth...*

From that yard, he converted discarded 55-gallon oil drums into a complete orchestra of steel drums. The steel orchestras he constructed and led, often overshadowed many of the worlds top conventional symphony orchestras. He led his first steel orchestra to the United States in 1965, where they broke all box office attendance records at the world renowned Radio City Music Hall. His name is Herman Rock Johnston and his band at that time was the West Side Symphony Steel Orchestra.

Later on in the eighties, he and my father formed a twelve member family band, which included my four brothers, some of my cousins, including my uncle's two sons, his wife and myself. The band, (The Johnston Fantastic Symphony Steel Orchestra), played mostly in the New York area and surrounding states. We played at Lincoln Center, The United Nations (with television personality Charlie Rose hosting) and at the Tanglewood Festival in Lennox Massachusetts (home of the world renowned Boston Pops) just to name some. Every time our band played we would receive countless standing ovations. The audiences would respond with tremendous applause as if they never wanted to stop.

Before he passed in 2001, my uncle said that our steel band (the Johnston family band) was the greatest band he ever had the pleasure and privilege of leading or playing with. We were simply musical assassins.

~~~~~~~~~~~~~~~~~~~~

***Spiritually**, my grandmother was at the pinnacle. She was undeniably at the mountaintop of spirituality. She built a small church in our yard where she* performed some of her miracles. She was the most spiritually powerful person I have ever known, or laid eyes on. To look into her eyes in my opinion, was the closest anyone could come to looking into the eyes of God. To me, she was the greatest manifestation of Godliness in a human being. Her name is Beryl Belfor, but we all called her Mama. She was not only a clairvoyant, but she was a spiritual healer and advisor. Her arms were always wide open and ready to welcome and embrace everyone. She too, was an extremely giving person. She was the supreme spiritual warrior that feared nothing. Along with my parents, she is my greatest inspiration.

I remember when I was about seven years old. I was playing in the yard with a friend, when she and some members of her church suddenly grabbed me and took me inside the church. I was kicking and screaming, but that didn't stop them. Mama and her posse (church members) proceeded to perform some type of ceremony on me. I remember them literally bathing my face with some type of oil while singing and chanting. I am not sure if there were any men present, but there were mostly if not all women in that dark candle lit church. At the time I just couldn't understand what they were doing to me and why. No matter how hard I fought they simply overpowered me and did what they had to do. Now that I've thought about it, it had to be some type of anointing.

*Throughout the years I could never get anyone to confirm that event, not even my parents. I started to believe I must have imagined it. But one faithful day as I was driving through Brooklyn New York, I ran into a childhood friend named Ray. As we sat in my car talking and the conversation got deeper, Ray suddenly turned to me and said, **"There's one thing I will never forget as long as I live."** I said really what's that? He then proceeded to describe the incident with my grandmother taking me into her church. I was so shocked I couldn't believe it. I felt so relieved and exonerated. I was elated! It was as though Ray was sent to reveal that truth to me. And when I think about it he was. Coincidence is not something I believe in.*

I must say I haven't seen or spoken to my friend Ray ever since that faithful day in Brooklyn.

Spiritually I am extremely proud to say, I have for the most part followed in my grandmother's footsteps, only without the conventional church.

(Approach)

The approach I've used to write this book is a spiritual one. Most of what you are about to read came from within my spirit, my Inner God. I purposely avoided using the opinions of external sources as much as I possibly could. The fact that our world has forever been plagued by war and colonialism, made it highly unlikely that our doctrine and our history can ever be trusted.

My hypothesis is that our spirit possesses infinite knowledge. The knowledge of all there ever was, all there is and all there will ever be. *So it makes perfect sense to tap into this pure and superior source, as opposed to a deceptive and biased one, that's assuredly inferior and contaminated...*

I actually spent a lot of my time lying on my back in a meditative state, literally staring up at the ceiling fan while writing this book. I've got to tell you, it has been completely enlightening for me, and I sincerely hope it will be the same for you.

(Purpose)

My purpose as I implied earlier in this chapter, is to complete the task countless people of goodwill have sacrificed their lives in trying to accomplish. People like Nelson Mandela, Bob Marley, Mahatma Ghandi, Martin Luther King Jr., Abraham Lincoln, Malcolm X, Mother Theresa, Harriet Tubman, John Lennon, Muhammad Ali, Marcus Garvey, Medgar Evers, John F Kennedy and his brother Robert: The list goes on and on.

Introduction

*Some may say I'm crazy. Some may say I'm arrogant. Some may even say I am a naive dreamer. To be honest, I am not the least worried about that. **Right now, I'm ready to Rise! Rise up and echo my message of peace to this world**... I refuse to accept the notion this world will never be at peace. I refuse to accept that we will never see an end to racism and bigotry. I completely reject the notion that we will never end hunger and poverty. I reject all these things.*

The world I envision is a world of love and peace where we are all united in our freedom. A World of enlightenment where we are healed of our psychological and social shackles, and is free of war, poverty and ruthlessness. I see a world of truth where people of goodwill are the ones making the decisions.

*My mission is to provide the enlightenment that will free us both mentally and spiritually. By dismantling the barriers that has for far too long kept us apart. I intend to expose what I perceive to be unhealthy and toxic **untruths** by showing how highly improbable they are; and replace those lies with intelligence that's far more probable **and closer to being truthful**.*

Though I am sure it's going to be extremely difficult. I truly believe this will be our time of liberation. Which is why I've made the pledge to be the voice of truth that unifies: The voice that will forever be on the side of peace, freedom and justice. I will be the voice of love that brings healing. I have made these things my life's purpose, and I absolutely intend to fulfill it. **So right now, I'm ready to Rise!**

Approximately seven years ago I received three divine words that not only beautified my consciousness, but also elevated it to an extremely high and simplified level. Every fiber of my being knows those words were placed into my consciousness by the divine **Creator** *of humanity.*

At the time, my son Nigel aka Rah and I was in my music production studio (situated in the basement of my home in Queens New York): As I was about to complete the music for a song I was working on.

I suddenly became consumed with an overwhelming desire to communicate with the Creator. A feeling like I've never felt. So I held hands with my son Rah and simply expressed thanks for our life and all the blessings we had received. Almost immediately I received this indescribably and unexplainably cool, calm, warm and powerful yet simple message of truth. Three words of truth that we all know but somewhere along the way have lost sight of its full depth and simplicity: A truth that has been maliciously contaminated by mankind's religious rewrapping of its purity. A truth I've embraced with all knowing and sureness as being the very essence of who our divine Creator is and who he has created us to be. Three words of truth, which I've used to pen the lyrics and title the track I had completed the music for on that faithful day in Hollis, Queens New York. Three words I now have the distinct honor, duty and privilege of reintroducing to the entire world. These three words in their exactness are: **"I Am Love"!!!**

One

The Healing Cry

(Let Healing Waters Flow)

"This love... This love that I'm feeling... This love is fulfilling... This love, this love is healing". There's nothing more fulfilling and healing to our existence than love. As is clearly highlighted at the beginning of this chapter: which actually is the chorus of my song "The Healing Song".

Love is the most powerful energy known to mankind. My hope is that this book will inspire the love that will heal us. True and divine love: The love that is the very essence of our peace and happiness. Not to be in any way confused with the superficial love we so loosely toss around like it's a rag doll. That love more often than not is based on infatuation and fantasy, rather than reality and truth.

Divine love on the other hand is a way of life. It is holistically rooted in reality and truth. Every fiber of *my existence knows this is the healing we so desperately need. Healing that will take us to a much higher plateau. Healing through love, truth and enlightenment.*

The truth is, we've all been so highly and maliciously desensitized, that our dysfunction has completely evolved into normalcy. We have been rendered blind to our shortcomings. This chronic blindness has made us resistant to the reality that we drastically need to improve the way we treat each other. In order to seek that improvement, we must first acknowledge there's a need for it. But the truth is, there are too many people who for whatever reason, choose to ignore the fact that we need healing. At least not the type I'm suggesting. Hopefully a bit of enlightenment might help to open up some minds and change some perceptions. So with that, allow me to enlighten you.

~~~~~~~~~~~~~~~~~~~~~

*If you believe your salvation depends on anything or anyone other than the love that abides within you, then I'll say you're definitely in need of enlightenment. In other words, there's no human being alive or who have ever lived that can ensure our salvation; and definitely not any religion or higher order either. Only love can do that. The love, kindness and compassion we need to have within our spirit; **nothing else!***

So I suggest we all start loving with every fiber of our existence, so that we can be healed.

~~~~~~~~~~~~~~~~~~~~~~

If you're impervious to the plight of the Native American Indians: The indigenous people of this great land, who as a result of Christopher Columbus' actions were heartlessly brutalized and slaughtered almost to extinction. Then I must urge you (out of a sense of pure decency and compassion) to get some enlightenment, so that you can be more sensitive and conscious of your fellowman's plights.

What's even more appalling is that Columbus continues to be celebrated annually as a great hero, yet there's no national celebration for what's left of his indigenous victims, The American Indians. I will say without a doubt that this definitely calls for healing and atonement.

~~~~~~~~~~~~~~~~~~~~~~

Understand! *If you're not sickened by or aware of the fact that the descendants of the Africans, who had been forced to endure over 400 years of the most vicious and brutal enslavement in the history of humanity, are still being blatantly oppressed as we speak; then you desperately need to be enlightened of the harsh realities of the unfairness that continuously reoccurs within our society, so that we can all come together and bring an end to this blighting injustice.*

~~~~~~~~~~~~~~~~~~~~~~

Anyone who for any reason is against efforts to prevent gun violence, following the devastating slaughter of twenty innocent children and six adults at the hands of a mentally psychotic individual in that Newtown Connecticut elementary school; Is highly in need of compassion, and lots of it! We need to come together and rid our society of this devastatingly crushing plague.

Let's talk about that faithful day in 2008, when Barack Obama and his family walked onto that Chicago field as the first family of these United States of America: If that event gave you no hope that this country is attempting to heal itself and you're not doing all you can to support it. Then there's no doubt in my mind, that you need to be more enlightened about the true history of this nation and its transgressions.

If knowing that 1% of the population may be actually wealthier than the remaining 99% doesn't make you realize that something is seriously wrong with this capitalistic system. I strongly suggest you get some enlightenment about the economic unfairness that's going on within our system, seeing that you're more likely to be a victim of it.

When an innocent young boy who was simply walking home with candy and soda in his pockets, can be viciously shot through the heart by a coward, psychotic want-to-be-cop murderer that racially profiled him: Only to have that murderer be completely exonerated by a court of law. I'll say we have a very serious and volatile problem, one that can be extremely chaotic if it's not rectified. Particularly when the murderer in this case, appears to have mercilessly ignored the boy's desperate and haunting cries for help; Then had the audacity to show no remorse by sadistically saying it was God's plan. This type of injustice and unfairness is a vicious plague on our society, and it has to stop. If ever there's a need for healing, this is truly one.

~~~~~~~~~~~~~~~~~~~~~~~~

If seeing homeless people sleeping on the street, or digging through the garbage for food doesn't make you wish you had the power to profoundly help them, then you probably need to be more compassionate.

What's more saddening, is that some of these homeless people are former veterans who have been broken by war. Broken because they probably had to witness the killing and maiming of fellow soldiers. Sometimes they are also burdened by the fact that they may have taken innocent lives, all in the name of an illusionary freedom. As a result of these veterans epidemic trauma, more of them are dying at their own hands than from combat. There's absolutely no question in my mind that this monumentally shameful situation, is over and above a cause for healing.

I've got to ask, are we really civilized? Are we even socially healthy? Is there equal justice for all? Are we truly free? I think not.

With that let's talk about freedom. When we have a bunch of arrogant and obnoxious hypocrites infiltrating our bedrooms and dictating to us who we should make love to and how many lovers we're allowed to simultaneously have; then we are extremely far from being free. When you have no freedom in your bedroom, it can't get much worse that that.

To be honest, when we can't even smoke a literally harmless joint without fear of being persecuted and/or prosecuted, when the legal stuff is killing us at a phenomenally high rate; then we are definitely not free. So I'll say it again, we're badly in need of healing. Healing through enlightenment and in some instances we also need atonement... So the question now is, how are we going to be healed?

Well! In my view there are 10 essential elements we need to have for us to be in a healthier place. The first two are love and truth. They are the ones that are going to enable us to acquire the remaining eight. Without love and truth it's a done deal, healing is impossible...

So let's start the process off with **Truth***. Truth is one half of the two major elements that's absolutely necessary not just for healing, but life itself. Without truth, nothing is real. Everything is an illusion, a fantasy, a myth, or simply a lie. So all those who can't handle the truth, I strongly suggest you get over it as soon as you possibly can. Immediately would be just fine. I'm not sure if you heard me. Nothing is real without the truth. There's no healing without truth it's impossible... So always try to embrace the truth without exception.*

The other half of the major elements and most important of them all, is **Love***. Love is the most important element of not just healing, but life itself. True and divine love. Love of self, love of God and love of humanity. Love purifies us. It illuminates our entire existence and strengthens it. It gives us that beautiful, warm and captivating energy. It is supremely powerful!* ***Having love as the consistent foundation of our everyday lives, elevates our relevancy to the Creator, and literally eliminates the need for prayer****. It elevates our spirit, or more definitively our Inner God. There's no way we can truly succeed or even survive without love, it is the key to everything. Love makes it possible for us to acquire the remaining eight elements. So make sure to never leave home without it.*

The next element is **Compassion***. Compassion goes hand in hand with love. It gives us added concern for* *the plight of others and prevents us from looking down on them. This ultimately leads to us having a stronger desire to help. So we should do our best not to leave home without it.*

   Humility! *What can I say; it helps to enhance the luster of our inner light. In the midst of adversity, it is often necessary to be humble. Depending on the severity of the situation, one might even be brought to tears. If that happens, just let it flow. Know that it is a good thing. Crying is a form of healing and it brings us closer to the Creator. In any event, we should always try to have humility at our disposal; we never know when we might need it.*

   Another frequently overlooked element we simply cannot do without is ***Forgiveness****. Lack of forgiveness blocks everything. There's no way we can achieve any semblance of purity without letting go of the anger and negativity that past transgressions against us can create. Without some level of acceptance and forgiveness, one can never be at peace, it's impossible! We don't necessarily have to forget, but eventually we must find a way to forgive. Hey! Love and hate can't occupy the same space. So all that debilitating anger we tend to store up inside must be eliminated. Love needs room to breathe. It has to be dominant. One thing love definitely cannot share is its power. Please don't misunderstand me, I'm not saying not to defend yourself when it's called for, that's not what I'm saying.*

I'm saying, when it is time to defend yourself, put humility in your back pocket and do what you have to do. There's evil in the world. Just don't hold on to that stuff, it destroys you!

*The next element necessary for us to heal is **Positivity**. It is imperative to have a positive outlook on life. Positivity helps to give us that all-important confidence we need in order to accomplish whatever we set out to. It helps to remove the doubt often fueled by fear. That's why it's equally important or even more so to avoid **Negativity** at all cost. Negativity increases doubt and inhibits us from accomplishing anything. Negativity often turns a normal situation into a toxic one. Even as an energy healer, you simply must get rid of all negativity in order to have any chance at healing. Negativity, other than serving as a clear warning, is always harmful and destructive.*

*Let's talk about **Balance**. Balance is key to all things. We must have a sense of balance in everything we do. Balance is what makes us moan with pleasure, as opposed to spitting out with disgust food that was cooked from the same ingredients. Balance leads to moderation, which always tends to be good, while imbalance can lead to extremes. Remember now, too much of a so-called good thing can kill you. So we all need to be conscious of balance.*

***Selflessness** is another attribute that contributes*

greatly to our healing. It not only elevates our importance, it also satisfies our sense of purpose and worth. In my opinion, giving of ourselves bodes very well for us in this lifetime and also the afterlife. Selfless people strengthen not only our community, but also our entire planet. We need a lot more of it.

The final 2 elements I can think of that contributes to our healing, is **Purpose and Passion**. We simply must have a strong sense of **purpose** in order to be truly successful in life. A strong sense of purpose can turn us into warriors. It gives us the drive to keep on going without ever giving up. It makes us do things with **passion**. Know that without passion there's no excellence. So whatever you do, make sure to do it with passion. In other words you must love what you're doing and try to do it as if you were born to do it.

This is a brief summary of my vision to get us to a higher place, a place of healing and enlightenment, where we can overcome our pain and suffering: A place where love and truth governs our entire existence. **Like you, I feel the pain, like you, I've cried many times. My sincere hope is that this book will be the healing water that flows from the tears of our pain.**

Two

The Art Of Deception

(Big Nasty Lies)

This chapter is crucially important not only to our awakening, but also our liberation. It sheds light on our psychological shackles and blinders and awakens us to the reality that we desperately need to eradicate them. It also awakens us to the reality that we are afflicted with a debilitating addiction to fantasy, fiction and sensationalism; One that we must overcome in order to find truth.

For far too long these obstacles have severely stunted our growth and prevented us from getting to the truth. Truths I firmly believe I can get us to once we're able to have an open mind. So it is imperative that you the reader have an open mind. Otherwise this book would not be of much use to you, at least not at this point.

It's unfortunate! But it seems like we're open to

change only when we are in the midst of great pain and suffering, and our current mindset leaves us without hope. So the best I can possibly do for those among us who are not that open to change, is to plant a seed of consciousness that could blossom at a later time. Hopefully, it wouldn't be too late.

Though the inspiration for this chapter came to me towards the end of me writing this book, based on the level of its importance, I've decided to make it one of the earlier ones you read. Considering you read this book in chronological order as I've recommended.

I can honestly say this chapter came to me at the height of my growth. So yes! Writing this book has been an extraordinary journey of spiritual growth and enlightenment. And I'm extremely confident it can be the same for you.

As a result of my growth, I've come to the stunning realization that almost the entire platform of our modern day western culture; is based on some form of religiously wrapped deception and trickery. Aka, **big nasty lies.** *These big nasty lies often in the form of fantasy, fiction and sensationalism have infiltrated virtually everything.*

It has infiltrated our history, our politics, our educational system, our religious beliefs, our social and moral doctrines, our capitalist structure, our sexuality and even our entertainment industry just to name some. We have been blinded to such a degree, that we have lost our true identity. This relentless bombardment of religiously wrapped fantasy, fiction and sensationalism, has literally transformed our precious planet into a fictitious battlefield.

I see a direct correlation between this book and the movie *The Matrix*. Which I'm sure you'll be able to relate to, seeing that it's a highly popular fiction.

If you remember in the original movie, there's a scene where Laurence Fishburne (who played Morpheus) gave Keanu Reeves (who played Neo) a choice between two pills, a red and a blue pill. If I'm not mistaking, I believe Neo chose the red pill. Well the red pill as I interpreted it, was supposedly the gateway to the spiritual realm, a realm of truth and reality where Neo was able to realize and develop his true powers and capabilities. A realm where he was able to see the world as it truly was.

This book in many aspects represents that red pill. I truly believe that reading and studying it would arm us with the ability to free ourselves from this debilitating web of nasty lies. Lies that has kept us in a fictitious world of flawed intellect and sensationalized religion, a world where our vision and capabilities are severely limited. This book is an uncomplicated Guide that breaks-through to a realm of spirituality, truth and empowerment, where our spirits can fly at impossible speeds and our vision and capabilities are innately limitless. This book will empower us to see things in their true light.

But in order to begin the process of liberating ourselves to this free and elevated state, these deceptive lies will first have to be exposed. ***"The truth is, these big nasty lies are so dangerous that they have created an avalanche of social toxicity and confusion; It is highly possible these lies can lead to the military annihilation of our entire world, particularly if international conflict ever gets escalated beyond a certain level".***

If you really think about it, when the foundation of any system or discipline is polluted with lies and sensationalisms; it means that the masters and teachers of that system have been educating us from the same flawed and contaminated source. Astonishingly, this appears to be the situation with some of our most educated and acclaimed people. This clearly indicates we have been raised on a wealth of false and misleading information that have been passed on from generation to generation. This is why we've been so confused and mired in toxicity; as is clearly evident in the results we're currently seeing in our society today.

If you don't believe me, just take a good look at our

world today. Is it getting any better? I would have to say in many instances it's not. Other than our technology, there are too many things that are seemingly getting worse. Socially, we've lost sight of what's really important; as we continue to be dominated by individuals who value pieces of paper (money) over innocent lives. It is getting harder and harder to find truly healthy food. And when we do, we can hardly afford it. Very soon, we'll be paying for high quality air to breathe. Selfishness have been on the incline, while community and family has clearly been on the decline. Economically, we are at the brink of Armageddon. The disparity between rich and poor is widening as we speak, while the middle class is rapidly joining the poor category. Do I need to go any further? Listen! In many aspects of our culture we simply need a new direction, and I'm ready to lead the change... So here's the raw truth; I sincerely hope you're ready for it.

The truth is, we have been systematically deceived, controlled and brainwashed by the continuous and abusive use of a religious rubber stamp. A stamp so powerful, every time it's used it turns the majority of us into robotic zombies. A stamp that has been empowered simply by the name it displays. And that name is God.

Unfortunately, this stamp has fallen into the wrong hands, and it has been recklessly and maliciously

used to instigate virtually every wicked and twisted deed that has been perpetrated against humanity. Anything that is stamped with this rubber stamp is attributed to God, which means it gets done no questions asked. This stamp even gets people to willfully commit suicide.

This religious rubber stamp has been used to demonize and destroy anyone or anything that dares to challenge it or get in its way. It has been continuously used to justify murder and genocide. This stamp has been used to socially contaminate us to the point of psychosis. It has been used as the fuel for bigotry and racism. This rubber stamp has been used to justify the forceful occupation of foreign lands and the brutal murder and enslavement of its indigenous people. It has been used to rally the troops and start practically every major war in history. One could argue, that this religious rubber stamp was actually used to start the British slave trade.

According to historical accounts, the first ship to transport Africans as slaves to the Americas was named (The Good Ship Jesus). A ship captained by England's Sir John Hawkins in 1562 who was a devoutly religious man. This religious rubber stamp has also been used to poison the natural bond between men and women. So much so it has driven an extremely destructive wedge between us, which is rapidly taking the conventional family structure to the brink of *extinction. There's no way of getting around the fact that every result has its reason, and every effect has its cause. To put it bluntly, this religious rubber stamp has wreaked havoc on our world, and continues to viciously do so.*

Three

The Inner God

(The Power Within)

*H*ave *you ever searched tirelessly for something only to find it had been on your person all along? Well! It has happened to me on more than one occasion and it probably has happened to most of you also. I guess that's what the great Bob Marley was referring to when he said the following line in one of his songs: "Meh belly full but meh hungry. Ah hungry man is an angry man". So in essence what Bob is metaphorically saying is that the wisdom and truth we've all been searching for innately exist in abundance within us. He's referring to the ever-elusive Holy Grail, Humanity's foundation of love and peace. The knowledge of all there ever was, all there is, and all there will ever be. All these things exist within our spirit. It is why we have the incredible ability to know the past and see the future, simply by tapping into our elevated consciousness. It's mankind's eternal reservoir of knowledge, wisdom and power. Unfortunately our inability to understand and embrace this truth is the root cause of our costly ignorance and chronic un-peacefulness, all of which we've learned.*

The major religions have simply been unable to awaken us to this powerful truth. In fact, some have actually gone out of their way to lead us away from it in order to control us. Making us weak, confused and needlessly dependent on their false doctrine. Well! It's time to end that...

The path to the Inner God is purely **spiritual**. *Spirituality is the only way we can get there. Many people mistakenly equate Religion with Spirituality. Which couldn't be any further from the truth.* **Your religion is what you've been taught to believe. It is more about the religion itself than you. Religion in many instances is a system of control, which takes you away from your true power and direct connection to the Creator. It often requires you to have a liaison to the Creator. It literally enslaves you. Making the liaison your master and not The Creator. On the other hand, your spirituality is about your personal power. It's about your spirit, which is your natural and direct connection to the Creator of this vast and seemingly infinite universe. It is about the God that already abides within you. You don't need any liaison other than love and truth. So please don't confuse the two.**

Love and Truth, *are the two most important keys to unlocking and developing this awesome godly power. Which brings to mind the title of another popular song, "Looking for love in all the wrong places". We have* *been virtually looking for love in all the wrong places, and without love it is impossible to find God, The God within!*

Well my love-starved earthlings our search is about to come to an end. Love is the divine road to our Creator and it begins and ends within us.

So what really is **The Inner God***? The Inner God is the spirit that has been liberated. It is the spirit at a magical and elevated state of enlightenment. It is the personal God we all have within us. I can tell you right now with all knowing and sureness, the Inner God is real. It is a higher state of consciousness. It transcends time, space and distance. It is the part of our existence that lives on eternally. Cancer or bullets cannot kill it. It's nonphysical and limitless. In essence, it is who we are. It is infinitely superior to our physical, and intellectual selves. It defies human logic.*

Although we all have it to some degree, some people appear to have it at a much higher activity level than others. They are the people that are more in tune with their spirit, more in harmony with it. I consider myself to be one of these people. It is for this reason; I am able to write this book. My love-based spirituality has enabled me to be the manifestation of wisdom and truth. When developed, **"The spirit is the greatest lie detector and truth finder that has ever existed"***.*

I have to say, many people don't seem to fully grasp the concept of the "Inner God". They don't seem to have the confidence or understanding to completely embrace the reality that there's such a high level of power existing within them. There are times I've spoken to people about the Inner God; and although they appeared to have agreed with what I had said, their following statements and actions told me they didn't fully get it. For instance, they might say: "You should come to my church and meet with my pastor, you guys are on the same wave length". Or they might mention something about Jesus or the bible; Not realizing they're attempting to take me backwards into religion, rather than forward into spirituality.

As I've previously alluded to, our spirits can reveal things long before they actually occur. We have the incredible ability to instantly know factual things about someone's past we had no logical way of knowing; Even though we are meeting them for the first time. We can also be aware of an illness they may have and the cause of it, simply by tapping into our consciousness. Amazingly! We can tap into these things from thousands of miles away. Personally, I have experienced many of these types of extraordinary, clairvoyant events; so have some of my clairvoyant friends. It is the reason why seers like Nostradamus are able to predict events lifetimes before they actually occur.

What I find amazing and unfair about the people that doubt our ability to see the future; is that they expect a seer to see everything without error. Although people see things with their naked eyes every day and completely misrepresent what they've seen. We need to overcome this negativity, in order for us to grow.

I recall one event that occurred prior to 2006: At that time, I was working on my then job in New Jersey. I distinctly remembered it being on a Sunday when I worked alone. As I was reclined in a chair in the dimly lit office overlooking the Hudson River, I suddenly had an overwhelming feeling that caused me to jump out of the chair. A feeling that led me to believe something was wrong with my nephew, who at the time was staying with his girlfriend at her mother's home in Florida. I immediately called the house where he was staying and a female answered the phone. With a frantic voice I asked to speak to my nephew, who's also my godson. The female said, "Who is this"? And I replied, "This is his uncle and his godfather, where is he"? I know it wasn't necessary for me to be so explicit, but I was for some reason. In any event, she said, "Why do you sound like that"? And I replied, "I have a feeling something is wrong with him". She said, "What are you, psychic"? I replied, "Sometimes! Where is he"? She then proceeded to inform me that he was on his way to the hospital. Apparently he was having respiratory problems. I took all the information from her and promptly relayed it to my brother (my nephew's father) who also lives in Florida. This is just one example of how extraordinarily powerful and important our spirits can be. I believe we all have this power within us to some degree just waiting for an awakening. Hopefully! I can help to trigger that awakening. So let's try!

The first step to awakening this awesome power is to acknowledge that we do indeed possess it, while dispelling any notion to the contrary. Once this truth is acknowledged, a commitment to make love, truth, positivity and compassion the daily foundation of our lives must be sustained. Combine that with some regular meditation and increased reliance on our spirit for guidance; and we should be on the path to awakening. This would also eliminate the negative and toxic hindrances such as jealousy and greed just to name some.

Increased interaction with people of a similar mind-set could also be very helpful. Your inner-voice should start becoming clearer and clearer, increasingly revealing all kinds of information and truths that will take you to higher plateaus. Your level of consciousness will increase exponentially. Eventually increased experiences of déjà vu will occur, prompting you to trust more in your visions and revelations. It is really a process of continuous growth, which takes you to a higher consciousness.

Hey! That doesn't seem too hard does it? The trick is to be consistent with the love and all the goodies that it brings with it. Eventually you will be purified of all your negative toxins, making room for more powerful energy and enlightenment to take root. Simple!

I know some of you may still be wondering why the leaders of the major religions haven't spoken more about the "Inner God". Well! If you think about it, the concept of the Inner God goes against what they've been teaching us, it is a clear contradiction to their religious agenda. It would put most of them out of business. There would be no need to go to their churches other than for entertainment if they got it like that. Why would you? You already have the power. Their teachings would only lead you away from what you already possess, your real power...

Frankly, these guys do more to confuse us than anything. Most of them are just ripping us off anyway. As I've mentioned before in the previous chapter, their flawed concept of God is a control mechanism that weakens us. It makes us easier prey. The moral foundation of our society is totally based on deception and lies. Lies that were put in place long ago by some very greedy and wicked people, the Hierarchy!

Please note! When I say (Hierarchy), I'm referring to the people that have been forever running things,

whether openly or behind the scenes. The people of wealth and authority who have always dictated the implementation of the laws and doctrine along with the information we've been embracing. The truth is, our social and religious doctrine has never been about our wellbeing. It has always been about greed and power, and still is.

These vultures figured out if they could convince us that their corrupted agendas were indeed the word of God, they would easily get us to believe and do anything without reproach. This has worked so well, it has proven to be by far the most successful control weapon in the history of humanity. As I mentioned earlier, this **religious rubber stamp** is the root of our confusion and dysfunction. So we really need to impartially challenge everything, particularly our religious teachings and beliefs. Once we do, we would quickly realize that most of the stuff we've been blindly following, needs to be discarded.

Religion has been the cause of some of the most evil and devastating incidents in human history. How could it be right? Something definitely has to be wrong with it. Just look at the results. Almost every war in our history has been triggered by religious differences. There's not enough love in the world; and thus far, religion has proven to be incapable of rectifying the problem. There is definitely a better way, and if you allow me I'll take you there.

So with that, here's my understanding of God and mankind's existence: Many people believe God is up there somewhere pushing all the buttons. I'm definitely not in agreement with that theory; it simply doesn't make any sense to me and I don't see any evidence to support that. If it were true, we would all be like robots without free will and we're not.

My feeling is that the spirit of man, is in some ways based on a similar concept to the spirit of God. (Apparently the belief that we are made in God's image and likeness is fundamentally true in my opinion, not on a physical level but on a spiritual one). Like God, our spirit has the ability to divide itself. So just as each of our children has our spirit flowing through their bodies, similarly, we all have the spirit of God flowing through us. So in essence, our Inner-God is what I call Divine Trinity (The unification of 3 spirits). Which are God's spirit, our fathers' spirit and our mothers' spirit. In that order! So these three spirits (Divine Trinity) combine to form the Inner God. They also combine to create the vehicle that temporarily houses it, the human body. This is the flow of life. This is the flow of our mortal (physical) existence and our immortal (spiritual) existence. Make no mistake about it! On a spiritual level, we are Gods!!!

So just as we all need to feed our physical bodies with the right foods in order to be healthy and strong.

*The food our Inner God needs to be empowered as I stated earlier, is **Truth and Love**; along with a few other things like compassion, positivity, balance and some meditation, just to name some.*

The meditation helps to remove the distractions from our consciousness. It enables us to hear our inner voices more clearly, giving us purer and higher thoughts. It is also why our dreams are so important. They come at a time when we have fewer distractions. The inner voice is extremely crucial to our existence. It is the best way for us to foresee obstacles or dangers long before we are actually exposed to them: As well as opportunities.

Just think about it, the seed of everything mankind has ever created came from the "Inner God". There were no books written to guide the creator of the wheel. He had to look within. That original idea came from his spirit, his Inner God. A great deal of the information in this book was manifested through my Inner God. As I said earlier, it is where every human being's true wisdom and power lies, within! It is the key to our liberation and world peace.

The truth is as I said earlier; we were all created to be Gods within our selves. It is the reason why we all have free will. If you really think about it, it makes perfect sense. If it were the other way around, then everything would remain as The Creator originally

created it. There would be no cars, planes or even cell phones. Bad things would never happen to seemingly good people. Obviously the external God would make sure of it. But it doesn't work that way. Why? Because we all have our own personal God we're supposed to rely on, our Inner God. How many times have you gotten the feeling you shouldn't do something, but you ignored it? Then you ended up regretting it. This happens all the time. We all get these premonitions. We simply need to develop our inner voice so they can become clearer and stronger.

But before we could totally trust in our inner voice, it is absolutely imperative we drown out our negative toxins by completely flooding our existence with love. So that our revelations will come from a more positive foundation, firmly rooted in love as opposed to anger and hate.

This will make us a whole lot better in every possible way. Obviously we would want to teach our children to do the same, which would then guarantee a much greater and better world for all.

The only way we can truly find inner peace is through our Inner God. So the more we start tapping into it, is the more peaceful our world and we will become. So know who you are so you can become your greatest self. Start loving, start meditating and remember to always embrace truth.

Four

360° Of Separation

(Let's Get Together)

*My understanding is that the creation of the human spirit is based on the unification of three entities: The spirit of God, the spirit of man and the spirit of woman, which I've given the name **"Divine Trinity"**. This divine concept of unification is the essence and foundation of who we are and who we're supposed to be as a human family, **divinely United...** I firmly believe this is what we need to aspire to for humanity to be at its very best. For far too long we've been divided as a human family, and it clearly has weakened us. For us to be stronger and more at peace, we need to come together globally in a just and harmonious way. Allowing the spirit of love (God) not religion, to be the foundation of this divine unification. The availability of the global Internet makes this unification highly possible and the time is now. Unfortunately, there are some people who would like us to believe this unification is not possible, as they do*

360° Of Separation

everything within their power to undermine it. They have been negatively exploiting our perceived differences in order to keep us all divided and at each other's throats. It is the old (divide and conquer) strategy. We are simply being used as pawns in their wicked and self-serving money games. We have been systematically brainwashed into senselessly disliking and opposing each other, simply to satisfy their selfish and sadistic desires.

When you really think about it, Symbolically we still exist in the old gladiator arenas of Ancient Rome, only on a much larger and global scale. We are being deceptively indoctrinated into different and often misguided gangs that are made to oppose each other. Whether it's through race, religion, nationality, sexual preference, political affiliation, gender or social status just to name some. We are literally being forced to pick sides and engage in mortal combat. It's always us against them.

*This is the vicious and malicious war that's consistently being waged against us. Unfortunately most of us are completely unaware of it. To say this is one of the world's great nemeses could be viewed as an understatement. It gives greater relevance to the quote, **"United we stand, divided we fall"**. This quote not only rings true internationally, but universally. My intention going forward, is to not only provide the intelligence necessary to expose the harmful barriers* *(the gang mentality I mentioned earlier) that forever have been separating us such as religion, race, nationality and so on: But the inspiration and guidance necessary for us to overcome our obsession with it.*

Overcoming the barriers will put us all on a clear path to healing our world and ourselves. I truly believe every human being can and will achieve some level of peace and greatness, once they can overcome the barriers that plague them. If these toxic and debilitating barriers are allowed to exist in their current state, we will never know lasting peace, personally or globally. So read on!

Five

Nature And Organics

(It's Got To Be Real)

*W*hat is nature? Nature is God and God is nature.
*Nature is the truth. It is the boss of all bosses. You
should never oppose or disrespect it. Nature should not
be ignored for any reason. If your first question isn't
what's natural, you're probably doomed to fail at
whatever endeavor you're about to undertake. Nature
is the conqueror of all conquerors. It is undefeated and
irresistible. All who resist it will be in constant
disharmony and never know lasting peace or
happiness. Nature is the Grim Reaper; it always gets
you in the end. Your body goes to the earth and your
spirit goes to the universe. Nature is God and God is
nature.*

**So even if you believe in the Big Bang Theory, in
my view it still is a production of (The Most High
Creator). In other words, whatever or whomever is
responsible for the creation of this universe is in my**

view (The Most High Creator). Hence making Nature the essence and manifestation of that creation.

In order to achieve the healthiest solution to anything associated with nature (which includes everything), nature should always be our guide. It should always be given prime consideration in our decision-making; there are no exceptions.

Nature is the sustainer of all life. It is everything in its true form and existence. Nature is the Sun and the Moon. It is the healthy air that we need to breathe without mankind's reckless contamination of it. Nature is the lioness that kills a dear for food, and not for fun or sport like we humans sometimes tend to do. Nature is the reality that life, as we know it must come to an end. Nature is the strong sexual desire sixteen year olds will have that legitimately needs to be addressed. Legitimate, because nature dictates that it is. Nature is an organic woman in the midst of ten handsome and available men, thoroughly excited by her choices: Hoping she finds that special one that blows her mind and could possibly be the biological father of her children. If ever she's blessed to have any. (Controversial? Probably! But true). On the other hand! Nature is also an organic man in the midst of ten beautiful and available women, thoroughly excited by the choices that he has, hoping and wishing that he could mate with all ten of them. (Controversial? Maybe, but it shouldn't be! Because

it's absolutely true). The man could also impregnate every one of those ten women at relatively the same period of time, while the woman could only be impregnated by only one of those ten men. Is this relevant? Absolutely! Is it controversial? Without a doubt! Why? Because we keep avoiding the truth...

So I'll say it again, nature is truth, and we better deal with it. Nature is the undeniable statement The Creator or Creators of the universe make in order to let us know what's healthiest and best. If we understand and embrace this truth in its fullness and its depth, life would be much greater and simpler for all.

Our insane obsession with monogamy is a perfect example of us stubbornly and arrogantly ignoring nature's guidance. Personally I see it as one of the most devastating plagues on our society. The attempted normalization of it has been consistently and viciously kicking our behinds. It has led to a whole host of problems, some of which we are completely unaware. "The fact that we like something and keep pursuing it doesn't mean that it's good or right for us. The truth is, there are a whole lot of things we seem to love that are clearly destroying us, and monogamy is definitely one of them. Let's face it, men don't cheat simply because they're bad, they cheat because they're not monogamous". So if you have any issue with this irrefutable fact, or need more clarification about it, I am quite confident you will get it when you eventually read the chapter titled; My one and only.

*It is very clear to me that this sort of insane denial of nature is at the root of our social failures. We keep avoiding the truth by ignorantly and recklessly overlooking what's natural and organic. Our absurd infatuation with fantasy and sensationalism has made us nuts. **Nature is our truth. Without this truth it really doesn't matter what the situation is, failure is imminent. It is as sure as the Sun that rises in the east and sets in the west.***

***Listen, it's more about what's organic and innate, as opposed to what we like. Nature should always dictate to humanity. We should always try our best to conform to it and not the other way around.** This is why we have consistently been loosing, and we will continue to do so until we learn to conform.*

So let me repeat! Unless we learn to have more respect and consideration for what's natural and try our best to embrace it with little to no compromise or interference, failure will be our destiny.

Nature and Organics are the keys to our mental, physical and spiritual health. It is the prime factor in our quest for inner peace and happiness. It is the guide to our best self. I'll say it again; it is our truth! Unfortunately, we've been fed a whole lot of concocted misinformation from way back in the ancient times. We've been consistently lied to, manipulated and abused. We are innocent victims of mass deception. So much so that we really don't know who we are supposed to be. We are totally lost and confused as humans. We're living in the "Jungle of the Lost", as one of my chapters is appropriately titled.

"When you alter the nature of any living thing, you've compromised that thing. You've interfered with its natural flow and evolution. Which takes it further away from perfection and causes much conflict. This usually leads to snowballing side effects that end up being much more harmful than beneficial". *Some examples are Monogamy as I stated earlier, Religion, Colonialism, Genetically Modified or Processed Foods, Slavery and so on. None of these things are natural or organic. The first two, religion and monogamy in my opinion are the main contributing factors to homosexuality. But if you also dispute this claim or simply need more clarification about it, you will have an opportunity to address it when you read the chapter titled: Homosexuality's Root. But please don't skip ahead to it. I urge you to stay on course and continue to read the book chronologically as I've recommended.*

*Historically, I place the highest priority on us knowing what our true nature and ancestry is. It is for this reason; I totally buy into the theory that **"We need*** *to know where we came from in order to know where we're going".* *The spirit of our ancestors vicariously lives on through us. Knowledge of them would help us to be more in harmony with our true selves. It could reveal some hidden talents, as well as some serious challenges we might encounter. Sadly... Our history has been contaminated to such a degree, that we really have no choice but to be very skeptical and challenge it at every turn.*

Scientifically, all paths lead to nature and organics. The more we learn about how to improve our health, it becomes increasingly clear that we should do and eat everything organically. Hey, I'm no food expert, but when I buy grapes, I always try to buy the seeded ones as opposed to the seedless. In my opinion it has a better chance of being natural. Natural or organic always seem to have the best result. You name it, breast milk for the babies, natural sun light, natural fruits and vegetables, natural herbs, conventional sex, walking, truth and the list goes on and on. All these natural things are better for us. We simply need to be conscious of balance; balance is key in most, if not all instances. We all could have the same ingredients in life, but the one that has the best balance will be the one who's healthiest and happiest. On the other hand, artificial and processed stuff is almost always bad for us. Not to mention untruths. All these things are not only making us unhappy, in many instances they're actually killing us.

How about some of those drug commercials on television? They are insanely insane. That's how crazy they are. There's one that supposedly helps cigarette smokers to overcome their habit, at the same time causing them to possibly have suicidal thoughts. Just the way they say it with such nonchalance, makes you believe it's merely a minor side effect. It's crazy! You could actually end up killing yourself simply by attempting to overcome your smoking addiction. I remember the first time I saw a commercial like that I thought to myself; this has got to be a joke. I couldn't believe they were serious. I was speechless.

What's also very disturbing is that some people are getting arrested for possessing marijuana, which not only seem to be virtually harmless but also helpful. While the real dangerous drug pushers are having free reign. It goes way beyond any thread of common sense and fairness to see that so many of these potentially deadly drugs are being approved, while a far less harmful weed such as marijuana continues to be unnecessarily stigmatized.

Obviously this has to be about the money. It seems like everything is more about money, as opposed to what's best for humanity. But what's even more sinister and disturbing, is that the criminalization of weed is blatantly being used as a means of terrorizing and incarcerating black people and people of color. This type of racial oppression and bigotry is completely wrong, and needs to stop, **Right now!**

Six

Jungle Of The Lost

(On The Road To Zion)

*J*ungle of the lost is actually the title of a song I wrote and recorded in 1998 that also featured an artist by the name of Mad Stuntman of the popular dance song "I Like To Move It Move It". So it's only appropriate I include my lyrics to the song seeing that this chapter was inspired by it.

Song Lyrics

Verse 1: *Rivers of blood have been flowing*
Millions of Lives have been lost
Masters of hate are increasing
The righteous among us are few
Believe in yourself, if no other
Got to be strong to survive
Too much pain (pain)
Too much sadness (sadness)
All this madness

Jungle Of The Lost

Chorus 1: *Living in the jungle (jungle)*
(Repeat 3 times)
Verse 2: *Nation of greed, nation of power*
Trying to rule this world
People of pain, people of color
Trying hard to survive
I wanna say, we are the heroes
But I gotta say, we are the victims
All I know is
What we need is love and
Understanding in this world today
Chorus 2: *Living in the jungle (jungle)*
(Repeat 2 times)
We're living in the jungle (jungle)
Jungle of the lost... Fighting, fighting,
Killing
Break: *We've got to come together*
In unity with harmony for victory
Let's come together (come together)
Let's help each other (Help each other)
Let's come together,
My people (come together)
Let's help each other (Help each other)
With unity yeah (repeat 3 times)
Stop the fighting; stop the killing
End this hatred
Tag: *Jungle, jungle of the lost*
(Keep repeating until the end)

~~~~~~~~~~~~~~~~~~~~~~~~

*J*ungle *of the lost is about the woes and wars that have been forever plaguing humanity that has caused generation upon generation of needless bloodshed. It is about the relentless brainwashing we've undergone that has not only stunted our growth, but has left us in a state of confused ignorance and blindness. So as a human family it is safe to say we are lost. For eons we've been plagued with too many unscrupulous lies. They are the seed of our brainwashing. **Anyone (other than the hierarchy who has had access to the truth) who believes they haven't been brainwashed is simply blind to the fact. Which is a very clear indication they're suffering from a more severe case of brainwashing.** There are some severely brainwashed people in our society that are holding PhDs and other forms of highly recognized acclamations. Due to their elevated and heralded status, these so-called experts are extremely dangerous. They are the ones who for generations have been consistently and arrogantly contaminating the masses with their flawed ideologies and bad information.*

Like pied pipers they are leading a great many of us to our doom. Their flawed teachings have left a vast majority of the people in a hard-wired state of blind ignorance. The situation is so bad, that many of their protégés (victims) are either unwilling or just incapable of embracing truth and welcoming positive change. Their hard wiring has become a habitual addiction and enslavement. Our western culture is structured in such a way that the final outcome we're going to be left with is a handful of winners and a majority of losers. **This heralded selfishness and greed is grossly unfair and blatantly evil. Too many people are literally spending their entire lives painfully struggling and suffering without any relief. There's absolutely no question that we drastically need to change our system.**

As we speak we are seeing nations on the verge of collapse. This is no accident; it is clearly a result of our flawed and crumbling capitalistic system. Again! Look at the results. There has to be a better way. Even our system of marriage and relationships are doomed from the get go. It has been a disastrous failure. It is very clear to me that we are in the midst of a civil war between women and men. This war has severely limited the amount of conventional families being started, and is rapidly destroying the remaining ones. It is truly a crisis of epidemic proportions: Of which most of the blame squarely goes to our religiously fueled monogamous exploits. Hey! I've got to place the blame where it lies. Our belief that monogamy is best has been consistently annihilating conventional families. Especially in the African American community, where the single parent household level is at a staggering 72%. This is a statistic I will be mentioning throughout this book. Why, because it is shockingly devastating. Black families are being systematically demolished as a result of our learned ignorance and psychosis.

Let's face it; monogamy clearly redefines our true nature. When you're not in harmony with nature you're definitely not in harmony with The Creator. Which means true happiness is an illusion that will never be realized; it's impossible!

Our only hope for achieving true success is to stop being hypocrites. We need to continuously seek and embrace the truth whenever we find it and reject the lies. In other words, anything that doesn't pass the smell test needs to be rejected. It's actually very simple! All we need to do is judge things based on their results, particularly our social doctrine and religious beliefs. Nothing should be off limit. We need to objectively question everything with an honest and open mind. Once we do, it will inspire the positive changes necessary to get us on the right track. I know in many instances I might come off as repeating myself and I most definitely will be doing so some more. To be honest I don't have much choice. In order to make my points there are some things that must be repeated, specifically when they apply to the topic at hand. Hey! I am attempting to undo over a thousand years of

brainwashing; so please bare with me and read on.

Seven

Love Is My Religion

(One Race One Religion)

*W*henever we choose to be faithful members of any religion and blindly follow it's doctrine with exclusivity (which is usually the case), regardless of what it is, it means we have chosen not only separation but in many instances enslavement. It means we've voluntarily blindfolded ourselves and placed ourselves into a box. A box that in many aspects is unnecessarily restrictive and harmfully divisive. Religion as a whole tends to be a quick fix that helps only in the short term, but in the long run it limits our power and weakens us. It takes us away from our true power (our Inner God), and convinces us to be followers of an inferior ideology. It often leaves us at the mercy of some very unscrupulous characters. Limiting us in ways that's unnatural and conflicting to our true and organic selves.

Religion is supposed to be the divine guide on how

to live and serve our Creator. It is supposed to get us to a state of oneness with our Creator and our self. It is supposed to be the road to our salvation. But in reality that's hardly ever the case. For starters, we've simply been bombarded with way too many different and conflicting religions. They can't all be the truth. So what is the truth?

The truth is, religion has too often been put in place and dictated by the hierarchy; and not God or any of his so called representatives as we are led to believe. In other words, it's just another form of deception and control.

A great example that supports my claim is the **Council of Nicaea** *that was held in the year A.D. 325. Reportedly this is where the Roman Emperor Constantine, dictated to the catholic bishops what the Christian doctrine was going to be. It is alleged that it's at this council, Constantine decided that Jesus be elevated to the same level as God or something to that effect. So many of the beliefs modern day Christians have been embracing is actually Constantine's doctrine and not God, Jesus or any of the religious leaders of that time. Religion on a whole is a learned discipline. A social programming and conditioning that in many instances lacks consideration for the truth, and blatantly insults our intelligence.*

Religion in my opinion is the most powerful and

deceptive system of control that ever existed in Humanity's History. The name of God has been deceptively used to justify a self-serving and corrupted man made ideology, one that has been consistently used to negatively control the masses while avoiding their reproach. This strategy has worked exceptionally well for a very long time. The powers that be has not only altered the truth, they've also created some elaborately fictional stories. These elaborately fictional stories and self-serving alterations have rid religion of common sense and mired it with contradictions. We literally have to be fools to believe some of the stuff they've been teaching us. It's brainwashing plain and simple, and it has been going on for countless generations. If we take the time to reasonably challenge the beliefs and teachings of the major religions, we will quickly realize they rarely add up. The results clearly bare that out. Anyone could tell you anything, but when the results don't add up, you have no choice but to question its validity. Which is a request I'll be making of you throughout this entire book. Question everything! Which is the exact opposite of what the religions require us to do.

Frankly! Religion has failed miserably in that aspect, especially the major ones. Yet many believers keep following them with fanatic blindness. This to me is incredibly senseless.

Religion in many instances has been used to

successfully divide the people of the world in a very negative way. It has clearly and undoubtedly been more about power and greed than God. To be honest, the bad things that have been caused as a result of religion have far outweighed the good. Religion has been anti freedom and anti peace. It has directly or indirectly led to murder, war, genocide, suicide bombings, racism, arrogance, sexism, segregation, selfishness, unfairness, injustice, hate, suppression, oppression, colonialism, ignorance, stupidity, weakness, insecurity, inferiority, fantasy, supremacy, intolerance, self deprivation, self degradation, hypocrisy, the demonization of sex, sexual abuse, slavery and the trivialization and contradiction of the concept of God itself.

These are just some of the problems religion has directly or indirectly caused. There's no wonder why more and more people are turning away from it, and who could blame them. Based on its history, it's a perfectly logical conclusion.

Honestly! The more I think about it, religion can be blamed for most, if not all of the world's social ills at the root level. It's like children having to live with bad parenting and abuse, and then later on in life finding out they've been adopted. Unfortunately many people have gone to their graves without ever knowing the truth.

I have to say, this is the perfect analogy with religion being the bad parent; and we all know what bad parenting can do. It could, and usually does mess up your entire life. The truth is not all religions are bad, but we don't have much of a choice in the matter if any at all. To choose or compare which ones are better would not fix the problem; it would only exacerbate it. Frankly, I think it's too late. I really do! The situation is much too contaminated and toxic to pick winners and losers. In my opinion, we have little to no choice but to set religion aside as a whole, downgrading its status on the grounds that it's too contradicting and discriminatory. Religion is like having a spiked punch at a kid's party, or an overly spicy batch of food only few can tolerate. You just have to set it aside and make a new batch everyone could partake in.

Now there're a whole lot of people who are going to say (You're crazy Black Warrior! How could you just set religion aside? It has done a lot of good and has continuously helped many people. There are a lot of followers depending on their churches and temples to guide them to salvation). My response to that is, we don't need religion to do these great things. All we need to do is come together and do them. The only thing that exclusively guarantees our salvation is love, and nothing else... Saying you believe in God, Jesus Christ, Mohammed or Buddha is not going to help you if you're not filled with love.

For instance: **Do we need to be Christian, Jewish or Islamic in order to be compassionate and kind to each other? Do we? Do we need to be exclusive followers of Jesus, Mohammed or any prophet for that matter to be good, caring and selfless people? Should a dying Jewish man be any more grateful to another Jewish person for saving his life as opposed to a Palestinian person doing exactly the same for him? The answer to all the above questions should be a definite and unequivocal no.** *Unfortunately, that's not where we're at, but we urgently need to get there; Like right now!*

We need to all come together under a unified banner. A banner that's simple and true that all humanity could easily agree upon. There is only one such banner that's capable of unifying the earth, and that banner is Love. *We really don't have much choice. If we truly hope to save this precious planet of ours, we must unite under the banner of Love. The spirit of Love is higher than every religion, every man and every prophet. Love of self, love of humanity and love of The Creator is the Holy Grail. In other words* **"The Holy Grail is Love! It's actually more important for us to fully embrace Love than to pray to God or verbally acknowledge him. Contrary to popular belief The Creator is not jealous or insecure; he doesn't need for us to be constantly calling his name. That does**

not fool him. If we want to be in his good graces what we need to do is love non stop".

We need to go forth in the spirit of atonement and forgiveness, under the divine banner of Love. This is the road to our salvation and the formula for peace. This is the solution. This is the Promised Land the great Martin Luther king Jr. was referring to. For it to become a reality we need to get to the mountaintop, and love will take us there. Like I said, the time is now. We can't change the past, but we surely can have a future as bright as the Sun. So I say to you! **"God is love and love is supreme. There is no higher praise you can give to God than to commit to living your entire life with divine love as your foundation. Love has never needed Religion, but Religion definitely needs love. So if you must have one, let love be your religion as it is mine".**

Eight

Jealousy

(What Is It Good For)

*J*ealousy, jealousy, jealousy! What can I say about it?
Other than it's bad, bad, bad... It's simply not a good
thing. Jealousy is bad in almost every conceivable way.
Let's put it this way, the instant you're jealous of
anyone, you are emotionally unstable to put it mildly.
But seeing I wouldn't be of much help to you by being
patronizing or misleading, I'll have to be bluntly
honest and say; once you're jealous, you are sick!!!
You are not well by any stretch of the imagination. In
other words, you need help.

   As far as I can see jealousy only serves two crucial
purposes. First it let's you know you're suffering from
an emotional illness that could become immensely
destructive; And secondly it let's you know you need to
find out what the root cause of your illness is and not
just the symptom. It is imperative you keep this in mind.
Too many people often make the mistake of thinking of

the symptom as the root cause. So I'll repeat, you need to find the root cause of your emotional illness and not just the symptom. But make no mistake about it; whenever you have jealous tendencies, you need to find a way to overcome ever feeling that way...

There's absolutely no need for jealousy in our world. It is completely unnecessary and toxic. Even if you're in a relationship that's not living up to expectations, you either come to an agreement and accept it in a positive way, or simply get out of it. But you're never supposed to feel jealousy. Once you do! Then the problem lies with you. It's that simple!

Jealousy is a very serious thing. According to how bad it is; it often leads to violent crimes, or even murder. It's no joke. I will even go out on a limb and say that jealousy is probably to blame for more violence crimes and murders that any other domestic issue. The way we as a society overlook jealousy as if it's not a big deal is mind-boggling and in itself sick. It's proof that we're not as civilized as we claim to be. To be honest! I don't think we're civilized at all... Jealousy has become totally acceptable in today's western culture. So much so that many people wear it as a badge of honor. It's not surprising that relationships are simply not lasting. How could they? We are already misguided as it is with our social doctrine. When you add something as toxic as jealousy to the equation, it makes it virtually impossible for *relationships to have any chance of succeeding.*

How many times have you heard preachers say, "God is a jealous God"; "Really! God is a jealous God? Who is he jealous of I would ask"? It is simply unbelievable the type of nonsense some of these guys preach to hundreds, or even thousands of people. It's utterly ridiculous! It makes absolutely no sense, and I'm being nice. They couldn't possibly be speaking about the Supreme God who they themselves claim to have created the Universe and all of humanity: The all knowing and all seeing (Most High Creator of all things). Of course not, no way! They've got to be referring to some weak insecure person who just happens to be named God. That's what it is! I must have clearly misunderstood. It has to be that.

Listen! These preachers are misleading the people and causing irreparable damage to their psyche. Subliminally intoxicating their social and emotional behavior. In other words, they're just making people sicker with their blatant lies and contradictions. When you convince people that God is a jealous God; you are in fact saying to them since God is jealous, then it has to be acceptable for everyone else to be jealous too. So in essence, these preachers are charging God with this lowly toxic emotion called jealousy, and subliminally encouraging the masses to embrace it also.

Don't get me wrong, not all preachers are preaching this nonsense, but the good ones (if there's any) need to call out the bad. We need to stop this madness. This reckless lying and ignorance seriously has to stop. Anyone who feels jealousy towards another person ought to be ashamed.

Listen my brothers and sisters; I want you to listen to me very carefully. I don't care if you had a billion dollar wedding in the Vatican, it doesn't give you ownership papers over that individual. I will repeat; you do not own that individual. When one person owns another person, it's called Slavery. And we all know how evil slavery is. Listen! **"One thing love is definitely not about is ownership (slavery)".** *So any ideology, mindset or ceremony that suggests or implies that one human has ownership of another, is simply wrong. It always leads to jealousy. No one deserves to die or be beaten up for choosing to do something with their personal life their partner happen to disapprove of. So anything in our society that encourages this mindset needs to be seriously examined, exposed and emphatically discouraged.*

There are basically two things that are at the root of our jealous mindset whenever they're compromised; and they are Love and Truth, the issues of this book. Actually whenever Truth and Love is lacking or compromised, they are at the root level of all of humanity's problems. Beyond that,

there is one main issue that's doing the most damage by fueling and justifying our epidemic jealousy. And it is the misguided religious belief that has for too long instigated the delusion that we're all supposed to be monogamous. The winner takes all ideology. This delusion is the devil of our jealousy dilemma. There are other things that help to fuel our jealous behavior, but I don't see them at the root level. Things like insecurity and also some of the visual entertainment that literally justifies violence against people who've allegedly cheated on their partners. You know the ones.

What's so crazy is that most, if not all of the afore mentioned things are celebrated by our society. Why is that? Why are we embracing and celebrating these things that have consistently intoxicated our existence? How have we allowed ourselves to come to this bad state? Does anyone truly believe we're supposed to remain this toxic? Or is there a better way?

We need to all ask ourselves these crucial questions and find the answers. Obviously something has to be wrong; otherwise the results would be a whole lot better. So we really need to find and accept the truth of this matter. *"Without truth, there's no real solution, it's impossible. So regardless of how painful the situation may be we should always demand the truth, nothing less".*

I have to tell you, the children are depending on us

to fix things for their future. But right now, we are seriously hurting them with our continuous ignorance. It's obvious they're feeling the pain. I know you've been hearing their cries? Come on be honest! As loud as they are, you've got to be hearing those screams. I can!

The bottom line is, there are too many obstacles that are hindering us in our society, and jealousy is definitely one of them. Jealousy is also blocking our ability to achieve inner-peace. You will never find a streak of jealousy in any person that possesses inner-peace. It's literally impossible. Therefore if we are to achieve inner-peace we must overcome our jealousies.

So what is the solution? The solution is, we first must completely disclaim any notion that jealousy is inevitable. We simply have to treat it like the plague that it is and stop embracing it. Once we do that we will have already won half the battle. The next step is to embrace the concepts of this book, particularly the main ones like love and truth. Once they are embraced, my readers will have all the tools necessary to overcome their toxic hindrances including jealousy. Hopefully we can bring an end to Jealousy; so read on!

Nine

Homosexuality's Root

(Is It Birth, Choice or Both?)

"Understand! For us to be liberated from this apparent sea of ignorance and deception we are drowning in; we must question everything. There are no exceptions. If what we believe is the truth, it should always stand firm whenever it's reasonably challenged. If it's not true, it will surely crumble into rubble when questioned with consistent impartiality".

"A foundation that's short on truth is flawed and destined to collapse whenever you attempt to build upon it. A life without a truthful structure is one with little to no happiness and filled with contention".

"Without truth there is no liberation, thus making inner-peace an impossibility. So in essence we all need to be liberated. Not through war and ignorance, but through love, truth, wisdom and understanding".

(I Got It From The Source)

As a result of the growth I've attained during my spiritual journey, some profound revelations have invaded my consciousness. Not to be presumptuous, but I truly believe some of these revelations could bring not necessarily a different prospective, but an added one to the plight of the gay community. I'm hopeful I will be able to provide a deeper understanding of homosexuality's root and possibly minimize the impact of the ongoing struggle. I also believe I can dispel some misconceptions opponents of the struggle may have. Which could lead to an even greater reduction in the amount of abuse and persecution gay people have been enduring.

Honestly! Writing a chapter on homosexuality was not something I thought I would be doing. If anyone would have told me a couple years ago I would be writing a chapter addressing issues on homosexuality, I would have suggested they be committed to an insane asylum seeing how volatile and sensitive I know this topic can be. But here I am!

As a heterosexual man I couldn't understand why some men would want to be gay much less be proud of it. I just couldn't relate to it. But my desire to always get to the root of situations (The Whys) has gotten me to this point.

I must say like President Obama, my opinions on this topic have evolved even before his allegedly did. But before I get into the meat and potatoes of this topic allow me to open up your minds a bit.

Though I truly believe what I'm about to reveal is both truthful and enlightening, I'm quite aware you the reader might not see it that way; And I'm perfectly fine with that. I just want you to know I'm not here to offend anyone. That's definitely not my intention. I know how painful differing or even truthful information can be. While what I say might not necessarily be a universal truth, I consider it much closer to the truth than some of the things we've been hearing. The great American Maya Angelou said something to the effect of: **"Whenever you learn you should teach, and whenever you get you should give"**. *In essence, that's exactly what I am attempting to do. I truly believe a deeper knowledge of one's self is always beneficial not only to the gay community, but to everyone. This, I consider being a universal truth. So let's get started.*

(The Tracks Of Their Tears)

If we really think about it, why would anyone simply choose to be gay? Why would anyone expose himself or herself to such persecution? Some gay people have even gone as far as to have sex change operations. The level of pain and frustration it would take for someone to even think about having a sex change operation much less go through with it, has got to be unimaginable. The fact that gay and lesbian youths are literally five times more likely to attempt suicide, is overwhelming evidence of how brutally real and painful their suffering is.

(Who's Gonna Take The Blame)

What's ironic, is that the people whose ideology and lifestyle I believe is the root cause of homosexuality, are the ones who appear to be most opposed to it. When in reality many of them are secretly gay themselves. I'm talking about the leaders of Christianity: Primarily those of the Catholic Church. I place the blame for homosexuality not on their shoulders, but squarely on their heads. Other than the food and drugs we consume, which I suspect is wreaking havoc on our hormones and overall health, I place the blame directly and indirectly on the Catholic Church. As they say, all roads lead to Rome, and in the case of homosexuality, I truly believe that it does.

(The Hidden Culprit)

It should be no great surprise that the Catholic Church is often viewed as being both the mother and father of homosexuality. This has long been suspected.

Now with that being said, I believe there's also a hidden culprit. A culprit in my opinion, which has triggered the infiltration of a child's sexuality while still in its mother's wound. That hidden culprit is **monogamy**... *Hmm! I know most of you are probably wondering what the hell am I talking about. Just bare with me and I'll explain everything in good time. Oh! Just to inform you! The Catholic Church is also the mother and father of monogamy, at least in my not so humble opinion. So read on!*

(Let's Go To The Video Tape)

According to historical accounts, during the early stages of Christianity polygamy was a very common practice throughout all ranks of the Catholic Church. Many of their clerics not only had multiple wives but also concubines. Even Peter, who's alleged to have been the first pope appointed by Jesus himself, was reportedly married with children. So with all things being true, this would clearly indicate that both Jesus and his heavenly father were at least cool with the clergy having Sex. Right!

In any event as time went on, the offspring that resulted from all that sexual freedom was causing the church to lose much of its properties. Apparently back then the priesthood was more of a hereditary thing; it was customary practice for clergy to pass the church's *property on to their descendants. This eventually became a problem as the Church felt it was losing too many of its properties and decided to do something about it. This led to the imposition of monogamy, and later on celibacy in order to rectify the problem. So these impositions that ultimately became official Catholic doctrine wasn't about God or Jesus Christ, they were about **Wealth**. Oh, excuse me! Let's not forget **Greed**.*

Apparently this triggered some extremely vicious and damaging propaganda by the church in order to justify its changes. So During the fourth century it is said the church's hierarchy began labeling sex as a sinful act. A cleric by the name of St. Augustine (A.D. 354-430) went as far as to state that an erect penis is a sign of man's insubordination. When you combine that with the belief that women will forever be cursed as a result of Eve's consumption of the forbidden fruit in the Garden of Eden (which is clearly a sexist myth). You have successfully demonized all of humanity. You have cursed your own and everyone else's existence. These views that have long fueled the doctrine of the Catholic Church are the most socially damaging in the history of humanity. This blatant demonization of both manhood and womanhood is the seed of our social confusion and suffering.

Without the erect penis of man (a huge blessing), getting together with the vagina of woman (a huge blessing), there would be absolutely no humans walking around. In fact, without sex (the greatest of all blessings), there would be no intelligent life whatsoever, including all those proclaimed (Men of God). As far as I know, none of them were immaculately conceived. Which would mean an erect penis is their genesis...

*This systematic brainwashing has caused us to dislike our true selves and each other. The stronger our belief is in this ignorance is the stronger our dislike of our organic selves become. **"When a people have been brainwashed into disliking their true selves, the obvious alternative is to become something other than themselves. This inevitably causes a huge amount of emotional and sexual conflict. For far too long we've embraced and recycled this brainwashing. Its devastating effect on humanity cannot be overstated. Along with being one of the root causes of homosexuality, it has also created a toxic an unnatural wedge between heterosexual men and women. The problem has further been exacerbated by the religiously fueled imposition of monogamy on society, causing a rippling effect through time. It has made us all the victims of the Catholic Church's insanity"**.*

When you listen to these proclaimed men of God you would think that sex was created by the Devil. Not that I believe in Satan, I don't! The belief that Satan is a real entity is a blatant insult and contradiction to the power of our Creator.

You should ask yourself, why would an all-powerful God allow Satan to have such power to wreak havoc on the world? In my opinion this defies good sense. This is why more and more people are turning away from religion and rightfully so. If there really were a devil, then it would have to be the concept of religion itself. Let's face it! Religions have triggered by far the most evil results in the history of humanity. When you maliciously demonize sex, the process necessary to create all intelligent life on earth, you are nothing short of being wicked, reckless, insane and even evil; And that my friends, is the undeniable truth.

(Is It Birth, Choice, Or Both?)

Well, that is the question. But before I answer it, I must say whether an individual chooses to be homosexual or is born that way is pretty much irrelevant to the legitimacy of the situation. The freedom to choose (and in this case our lovers) is what a free society is supposed to be about. There's absolutely no reason on God's earth for the government to interfere with the bedroom habits of consenting adults. It is clearly an infringement of our civil rights and every other type of right you can think of. To be honest, we shouldn't even be having this ridiculous   conversation.   Homosexual   and transgendered people deserve all the rights to be just as miserable as the rest of us.

With that said, let me answer the question of whether homosexuality is birth or choice.

*I will have to somewhat disagree with people such as Lady Gaga who believe homosexuals are born that way and say; Some people are born with a **(Higher potential to be gay)**, but there's always a choice: However, the choice is much more difficult for anyone with a (Higher potential to be gay) regardless of how they got there. Whether it's through birth or sexual abuse. But all in all, there's always a choice, although not very much of one.*

*Now! To answer the billion dollar question as to what causes some individuals to be born with a (Higher potential to be gay), it is imperative that we understand that **"Our sex is determined at conception or soon thereafter; but our sexuality is developed and influenced during the period following conception, which extends to birth and beyond"**. So the crucial period following conception is where I believe the emotional, psychological and spiritual state of pregnant women greatly influences the development of their unborn child.*

Although I believe both parents have something to

do with it, I'll say the mothers bare the brunt of the responsibility.

In any event! Due to the epidemic failures of our society's monogamous exploits, many pregnant women often harbor negative feelings not only towards the fathers of their pending child, but the male species as a whole. So when that happens, my feeling is that the negative energy could be subconsciously transferred onto that developing child. Remember now! We are spiritual beings. The spirit governs our entire existence. When the body dies the spirit still lives on eternally. Our spirit or more definitively our Inner God is who we really are. It controls us. So let's say a woman is having a son, the negative energy she may have within her spirit towards his father, could affect her unborn son in a way that emasculates him. She could be hoping and praying the boy is nothing like his father, totally unaware she's increasing his chances of becoming gay. The same could be true if the woman is having a daughter. The negative energy she may be harboring towards men could transfer onto her daughter, possibility causing the child to be born with an inherent lack of appreciation for manhood and also a disdain for the reality and plight of womanhood. Thus increasing the daughter's chances of becoming a lesbian. The truth is, most earthlings are totally unaware of the powerful impact energy can have on us, both from a positive and negative standpoint. As someone who's into energy healing I understand the importance of energy (oh so well).

Too often in today's society our prevalent negativity continues long after childbirth, and is transferred onto our children. Which further increases a child's chances of becoming not only homosexual, but also conflicted and troubled. One could argue that this is a natural evolution of the social doctrine, which has long been implemented by the Catholic Church. And right now, I am making that argument.

(Don't Blame Me For Being Lesbian)

I remember a female friend of mine who wishes to remain anonymous, telling me that before she met her husband she was seriously thinking about becoming a nun. Apparently her mother along with other female relatives had consistently bombarded her with their stories of how bad men were. The negativity was so bad; she wanted absolutely nothing to do with men. Fortunately, through the help of some friends she was somehow able to overcome the negativity and find a suitable husband. Many women are not that fortunate: Not only to overcome the negativity so prevalent in todays society, but also to find a compatible mate. When you combine that with the fact there's a shortage of available men and a social doctrine that literally mandates that women have a monogamous relationship with that one special man; it obviously leaves a whole lot of women out of the heterosexual equation. So it's only natural and understandable for many of these women to turn to lesbian activity, or become mistresses. Sometimes even both. Who could blame them? Like I said, all roads do lead to Rome.

(Why Are We Here)

"The sexual bond between man and woman is truly a divine gift from our Creator. It produces the most beautiful, organic and sacred result known to mankind, new life. It is mankind's highest purpose". It is the main reason we are here, which is to insure the continuation of human life. It is also why an orgasm is the sweetest feeling known to mankind. This is clearly by design; it has to be. If you really think about it, it makes perfect sense. The sweetest feeling, is what fulfills the highest purpose, New Life... It is very obvious to me, this process was carefully orchestrated, and whoever created us definitely wants us to have sex, and lots of it. This is my truth. This is why I know mankind was created by a higher source. What do most people (including atheist) say when they're having an orgasm? Oh God! I rest my case.*

(We've Got To Have It)

Although the main purpose for sex is procreation, it

has many other very important benefits. It's highly beneficial to promoting health and sustaining balance, not only physically and mentally but also spiritually. The importance of having that sexual release cannot be overstated. It actually helps to reduce stress, and extend our lives. My feeling is that whenever we have an orgasm, we've pretty much experienced a piece of heaven. So when the conventional method of having sex is deprived or unavailable, many people will naturally resort to alternative forms of sexual gratification. Whether it's masturbation and or homosexuality. They simply need to have that sexual release, that orgasm. This is why I believe the Catholic Church's rule mandating lifetime celibacy for all clergy, has made it the main breeding ground for homosexuality and pedophilia. With all the suppressed sexual desires these people must have been harboring, it's only natural for them to crave sex. Hey! It's nature, and nature wins out every time.

*It is said that many of the church's hierarchy including some popes were active homosexuals. I am not sure exactly when altar boys were introduced into the Catholic Church. But one could only imagine the amount of sexual abuse that occurred throughout the years. It has got to be staggering. My theory is, **"if you alter the nature of any living thing, you've compromised that thing. You've interfered with it in a way that could change its natural flow and***

evolution". *So it had to be extremely difficult for all those abused altar boys not to become homosexuals. Apparently the Catholic Church has been guilty of these atrocities for hundreds of years.*

(The Victims)

So this is where we are. It seems we have all been victimized and preyed upon by the corrupted system of some very greedy, perverted and power hungry men: A system of which the agenda has been to deceptively control us. A system that has severely weakened us and kept us divided and enslaved both physically and psychologically: Straight against Gay, Black against White, Christian against Muslim, American against Asian, and Man against Woman. I think you get the point. It's all about separation, 360 degrees of separation. The bottom line is, we need to come together in peace and respect each other's right to be free. Freedom to love whom ever, how ever and how many (consenting adults) we choose. My advice to everyone is to be honest with you. If you're able to be at peace with your sexuality, by all means embrace it with all fullness and positivity. But if you're not, then don't be afraid to pursue change. We should all do what's best for our spirit and not anyone else's. At the end of the day it's all about freedom. With love, truth, positivity and spirituality as our foundation, anything is possible. Just be careful to stay away from the religious fanatics, and remember that freedom means we don't own each other. It is imperative we all remember that.

In closing, I sincerely hope I was able to be helpful. To be honest! The majority of us are just innocent victims anyway, and I definitely don't see the God of love punishing innocent victims. Do you?

Ten

Balance Is Key

(Too Much of A Good Thing)

*B*alance is essential to all things. Everything we do requires some sort of balance. Balance is the difference between licking your fingers during a meal and making an excuse to go to the bathroom to throw it all up, even though both meals were made with simply a different blend of the same ingredients.

To say that balance is the key to our mental and physical health cannot in any way be overstated. Some sort of imbalance is what causes most if not all mental breakdowns: Likewise, most types of physical illnesses. There are people who've smoked tobacco and drank alcohol for basically their entire lives that have almost made it to 100 years of age, some actually lived past it. Not to overlook the fact that you probably should avoid smoking tobacco altogether, but to make the point as to how crucial balance is.

Balance is also the key to greatness. You cannot be great at anything without having great balance. Wherever there is true greatness you're sure to find excellent balance. They go hand in hand. A great example of this is NBA basketball player Lebron James. He is by far the best balanced of all the top players, hence why he is undoubtedly the greatest player. Everyone has to create their own balance within his or her innate capabilities and limitations. What works for one individual might not work for another. In order to find true balance one needs to tap in to their spirit. Each individual's spirit or Inner God is vitally important towards creating their best balance. It is virtually impossible to have anything close to a well-balanced life without being in tune with your spirit. Balance keeps us in harmony with nature and the Universe. It is extremely crucial in determining the quality and length of our lives.

In order to maintain great balance it is always good to avoid extremes and do most things moderately. In most instances, it's not what you do but how much you do it. Too much of a so-called good thing could kill you. Always remember that.

Anyway, I think you get the point. So with that let's change the vibe and lighten up the mood a bit, seeing that we are speaking about balance. Let's see! What topic can I address that's going to balance things out? Oh! I think I've got a good one. Let's talk about (The

Art of Making Love). That's actually a great one. I don't mean to boast, but I think I know a little something about the topic; at least from a male's prospective, seeing that I'm known globally as a great lover. Don't laugh I'm serious! You young guys better take some notes. So here goes!

~~~~The Art of Making Love ~~~~

Ok! Stop laughing and let's get serious! Why don't you come a little closer so I could speak to you privately? First I want to let you know I'm not here to embarrass you or hurt your feelings in any way. But I must tell you! I happen to know you're in need of some assistance in the lovemaking department. Let's not get into how I know but I do. Hey don't feel too bad, you'll be surprised to know how many people are in that same club you're in. The truth is, there are far too many people who are lacking in the lovemaking arena and too few who've mastered it. So if you don't mind, allow me to share what little expertise I have in this area with you.

Fellers! Let me start off with you. The first thing you guys need to do long before you get naked with that woman is massage her mind. Make love to it in a very sensual way. That's where the female's orgasm starts. Use soft deep tones if you can and try to make her laugh. If you're able to accomplish that, then everything you do from that point on is likely to have a much greater effect. You definitely shouldn't have too much of a problem in getting to the Promised Land especially if she's genuinely interested in you. And depending on how good you are, when you do get to the Promised Land both parties should be enjoying a beautiful taste of heaven if you know what I mean. But before you get physical try not to have too many pre planned moves. Just take it slow and go with the flow. Understand! In order to be a great lover you need to find the best balance for each separate occasion.

Making love is a highly spiritual thing. More than anything, it's an exchange and intermingling of energy that can be magical when it's right. So you need to feel the spirit of that woman in order to be in harmony with her and vice versa. *You need to know when to be firm and when to be tender: When to be slow and when to speed it up. You need to find the right rhythm, the right balance. As I previously said, balance is the key and it always applies.*

When it comes to making love you need to have passion. Regardless of what you do, you should always do it with passion or don't do it at all. Passion touches the soul. It can produce an orgasm from almost any body part. *Hmm! You guys seem extremely quiet now, I wonder why? Anyway, always try to feel the depth of what you're doing, and remember to have* *fun. If after you've made love to your woman you feel compelled to check her pulse, you can safely say you've done an excellent job.*

Oh! I almost forgot; there are a couple more things I need to mention. Whatever you guys do, try not to be overly affectionate in public; it can be anti climatic. By the time you get to the big showdown, a great deal of the excitement is gone. So save something for the bedroom or wherever the final scene is going to go down. And I will repeat, take it slow. Take it slow to the point that she's almost begging you for it. Trust me when you do that, she might be going to heaven multiple times...

Ladies! *What can I say, I guess the same thing goes for you, so whatever you do you should do it with the 3 Ps, pride, passion and positivity. It's not acceptable for you to just lie there and look pretty, especially when the relationship is past the incubation stage. Too many of you ladies have the wrong idea. You think because you're giving up the pie your work is done. That mentality will guarantee your man not only cheats on you and fast, but also replaces you if he's prompted to: Seeing that you're likely to be in a so-called monogamous relationship where he is required to only partake of your pie. So here's a tip! If you want to make it much harder for him to want to cheat, and ensure that he will never want to leave you.*

Whenever you're making love with your man, you

*should perform like you're auditioning for a starring role in his XXX romantic movie, knowing that there's a bunch of women waiting in line to audition for the same role; and when you're finished auditioning (making love), your man should have no choice but to send everyone else home. Remember, it's your responsibility to arouse and stimulate your man. And when you put everything into it, you have the extraordinary capability of getting an orgasm even when you're simply pleasing him. **Listen! If he thinks your talents are that of an experienced high price professional, it should be a great thing in his eyes.** If that's the case he's going to want to be with you for life. If he has a problem with it then he's probably damaged goods.*

Sexually, most men are likely to need some form of guidance. As long as it's done tastefully it's cool. Hey! Sometimes you have to let your man know what's working and what's not. But whatever you do try not to bruise his ego too much. Men are more fragile than you may think. Know that ego is a very necessary part of manhood. The damage that a bruised ego can inflict could sometimes be irreversible. It is also imperative you understand and embrace the reality that sex is naturally at the top of every man's list. If your man doesn't appear to be paralyzed or in a coma after a love making session, you might have a major problem; But if he does, you can confidentially know that you've done your thing and done it Well... So have fun, heaven awaits you!

Eleven

True Prayer

(Stop Reading And Live Right)

*W*hat *is Prayer? Is it really relevant? Is God truly listening? And if he is, will he respond? Well! From my perspective, I'll say it all depends on whether you're deserving of his blessings or not. If you're not, what you perceive to be a blessing is likely to be a curse rich with materialism, misery and emptiness; and if your stubbornness persists, your misery may follow you into the afterlife either prematurely, or after a long life of materialistic hell...*

Prayer is supposed to be an honest, humble and unscripted communication with The Most High Creator. It is supposed to be from your heart. At the end of the day sincerity is a must. If you're not sincere, regardless of how long and hard you pray I would say you're wasting your time.

Many people read from religious books like the

Bible or Qur'an when attempting to pray. In my opinion when you do that you're actually reading not praying. Don't get me wrong! Reading from these books can be extremely enlightening and motivating, but I'll have to say it's not praying.

When you do pray, whether it's verbal or telepathic, you're in a sense praying to yourself. The reason I say this is because I truly believe the spirit of God is within us all. So in essence, the answers to all our prayers lie within.

The way I look at it! **God gave us all a personal encyclopedia and crystal ball in the form of our Inner God. As I mentioned earlier, it has knowledge of all there ever was, all there is and all there will ever be.** So I would think it makes all the sense in the universe to tap into it, instead of religiously praying and asking for all sorts of things out of ignorance. After all, your Inner God is part of you, so why wouldn't you use it?

Let me ask you this question: If you were being beaten to death by a thief you've discovered in your home, and you had a very powerful weapon on your person, would you use it to defend yourself, or cry out for help hoping that someone hears you?

When you really think about it, that's pretty much the same situation we're all in; We are being heartlessly controlled and beaten to death by some *very greedy and unfair thieves; And all we have to do to free ourselves and overcome them, is to tap into our Inner God as we come together under the divine banner of Love, while we fully embrace it within our selves... But so far we're not doing that.*

For argument's sake, let's assume I'm completely wrong about the Inner God and the religious practitioners are correct with their beliefs and ideologies. I would think whenever you pray to God asking for stuff, you are in fact telling (The all knowing, all seeing Master and Creator of all things) that you have made a personal judgment on your needs as opposed to relying on his judgment. Which in my opinion would be a blatant contradiction. It seems to me even from a religious standpoint; once you sincerely acknowledge the Creator and are truly thankful for all the blessings bestowed upon you including life itself. That should be enough to cover you, considering you're repentant (asking for forgiveness) about unjust things you may have done out of ignorance. Maybe then you could follow that up by asking for some guidance. Making sure everything is sincerely coming from the heart. Now that should truly cover everything as it pertains to you. I would definitely say you're done... Oh! Wait a minute! That's providing you commit to being a kind, loving and compassionate person for the rest of your life. Otherwise you've just wasted your time. Confused?

Think about it! Why would the God of Love help someone who's not fully committing to love? So in my opinion, you could pray until you're blue in the face it's not going to help you. Like I said, any perceived blessing is more likely to be a curse rich with materialism, misery and emptiness. **The bottom line is, we've got to commit to Love**.

What really disturbs me is the hypocrisy of some religious people. The ones that regularly go to church appearing to be staunch believers in whom they perceive to be God; Many of them could recite passages in their Bible or their relative religious books without even opening it. But if you carefully study them, you quickly realize their way of life is lifetimes away from them being righteous. So what's the use? It is as though these people somehow believe they can fool the Creator. It's kind of laughable when you really think about it.

With that, let's talk about confession. **I firmly believe going to church and confessing our so-called sins to someone who in all likelihood needs forgiveness way more than we do, is utterly ridiculous. Confession in my opinion was the N.S.A of Ancient times. It was more of a ploy the Catholic Church used to deceptively spy on the people. It was all part of their system of control. So all those people who believed they were confessing to God or Jesus was unknowingly confessing to representatives of the** *hierarchical establishment. In other words, they were confessing to sinful spies. To be honest, the entire process was sinful and still is. Even the concept of Jesus dying for our sins, is untrue and destructive with its implications. In my opinion, it actually encourages so-called sinful behavior when we believe our sins can be so easily washed away. The truth is we are all accountable for our sins. We need to know we can't be demons for 6 days and 23 hours of the week and hope to pray it away in 1 hour: Only to go back to the same routine. It simply cannot work that way.*

"Spiritually or otherwise! For us to truly receive blessings, we need to live right and be right for 24 hours a day, 365 days a year for the rest of our lives". That's the only way.

In other words, prayer is not really as relevant or even as necessary as we think it is. At least not in the way we look at it (reciting words). At the end of the day, the only things that matter are our actions and our energy, not our words. "One honest act of love and kindness is lifetimes greater than reading a million bibles or reciting a million psalms. But the greatest prayer is based on our way of life. It is based on how righteously we live our lives in the eyes of the Creator. So if we truly try to live each and every moment of every day with love, compassion, kindness, truth and thankfulness as our foundation, our lives would be the greatest prayer. It will bring us Closer to Truth, Closer to Love and Closer to our Creator". So in essence, "True Prayer is being thankful and grateful for life; consistently living it with love, compassion, kindness and truthfulness: Not just some days, but every day until our life journey is complete. This sacred commitment will enlighten and empower our Inner God to divinely lead us on a path of righteousness. Harmoniously transforming our entire life and ultimately our entire world into a True Prayer". It's just that simple!

Twelve

Emotional Insecurity

(Mirror-Mirror On The Wall)

*W*hat can I say about emotional insecurity, other than it's a very bad thing, especially if it's at a full-blown level? Emotional insecurity is an extremely harmful affliction. It is a major obstacle in our quest for inner peace. **"Chronic emotional insecurity is a hungry beast that cannot be satisfied by anyone. Not your partner, not your friend, not your religious leader, not your psychiatrist, not even you can satisfy this beast. It is impossible to satisfy it. The more you feed it is the hungrier it gets. It is a gluttonous parasite with a bottomless pit for a stomach".** It literally blinds anyone who suffers from it. It makes it virtually impossible to see things as they truly are. A simple compliment paid towards someone who is emotionally insecure can easily be seen as a brewing plot or an insult. Normally harmless jokes can be quickly interpreted the wrong way. Emotional insecurity makes it almost impossible to completely *trust anyone, including yourself and definitely not your romantic partner. Without trust of self, there's no way you could possibly trust your partner or anyone else. Which means your relationship eventually become toxic and is eminently doomed. It makes very little to no difference how good or tolerant your romantic partner is, it only prolongs the inevitable.*

Emotional insecurity breathes the air of negativity. It inhibits us in many different ways. It blocks our happiness and greatly contributes to chronic frustration and depression. It can also sap our confidence, making the achievement of success much more difficult. In fact, even if we happen to achieve success, it is often very hard for us to see it that way. Emotional insecurity can often lead to chemical or drug dependency. It can turn anyone that suffers from it into a hopeless stalker and lowly spy: Always snooping and digging to find evidence to justify their manufactured suspicions. It is a life filled with contention, which often leads to misery, gloom and jealousy.

Emotional insecurity can be extremely challenging. However, it is quite possible to overcome it, and whenever one does overcome it, they are firmly on the path to becoming a warrior. I know! Because I've had to personally overcome it.

The only way to overcome emotional insecurity is

to beat it into submission and destroy it. I know it sounds pretty intense and graphic, but you need to remember you are dealing with an unrelenting beast. So you literally have to annihilate it by consistently flooding your existence with the spirit of love and compassion both internally and externally, which leads to the development of your inner power and consciousness. Be grateful for life and all your blessings.

Eventually you will have a greater appreciation for what's truly important in life as your confidence steadily increases. Your new awakening will ultimately drown out your insecurity. Leading to the manifestation of your inner beauty and power. I've got to tell you, inner beauty is true beauty. It is not only ageless and timeless; but its powerful brilliance is illuminating to your entire existence.

We need to understand that external beauty is only an opinion. It's something that is both superficial and temporary that's destined to wither. We need to focus our attention more on being beautiful internally and with our actions, and appreciate others for doing the same. Once we do, insecurity will hardly ever be a problem. Other than that, the best advice I can give to anyone who has an issue with emotional insecurity is to read this book. I am extremely confident that anyone who embraces the major concepts of this book; will eventually overcome their problem with emotional insecurity like I've had to. So have fun!

Thirteen

My One And Only

(Monogamy Vs. Polygamy)

*W*arning! *If you believe your views on the current topic of discussion is the truth and you're against any opposition of it, I strongly suggest you skip this chapter. Otherwise proceed at your own risk.*

But before you do, I would appreciate it if you follow these instructions:

Raise your right hand and place it over your heart while repeating these words. **"What I'm about to discover is the truth, the raw truth and nothing but the truth according to Black Warrior, so help me God".** *Remove your right hand from over your heart and relax. Now take a deep breath and read on.*

We've Been Wrong For Too Long

Let me start off by being completely honest with you

and say: *It simply has taken us Western Earthlings way too long to figure out our monogamous dilemma. The fact that it's 2014 and we haven't come to terms with this dilemma is nothing less than shameful. To put it bluntly, we have ruined way too many lives with our downright ignorance and stubbornness. Our inability to deal with the realities of monogamy is irrefutable grounds for downgrading our social status from intelligent and civilized, to confused, clueless and self-destructive. We have been in a constant state of denial. Monogamy has forever been nothing but a myth. It has failed miserably and shows absolutely no signs of ever getting better. Yet we keep relentlessly pursuing it. If there were one word to describe the situation, it would be* **Disastrous!**

With that, I'm going to valiantly attempt to bring our confusion to a swift end with this one chapter. So bear with me.

The Problem And The Solution

Let's get right to it! **Emotionally! Monogamy seems to be much more in harmony with the ladies. You ladies clearly have a stronger desire for it. Which makes it much easier for you to be monogamous. The problem is men are the opposite**. *It seems to me when you ladies love, it's so intense; it literally is impossible for you to love anyone else when that love is true. On* the other hand guys are not really that way. If allowed, we are quite capable and comfortable of truly loving in surround as opposed to mono like you ladies. That's actually the gist of it. I can't tell you how many times I've heard women say: **"If he really loves me how could he cheat on me"? The truth is, we can and we do. Why, because we are different emotionally. It has very little if anything at all to do with the love we have for our mates. Listen, the law of equality simply does not apply emotionally to the nature of men and women. Whenever you refuse to accept that fact and try to change it, you run into a whole host of problems. You cannot recklessly alter nature without severe consequences; it is what it is and you must respect that**.

Monogamy has never been compatible with manhood, and frankly I don't see any hopes of it ever being. Personally! I have never met a truly monogamous man in my entire life. Not even homosexual men are monogamous. So ladies, how could you possibly hope to have a completely monogamous relationship with someone who's never been truly monogamous? The supply of truly monogamous men on planet earth is zero to none; at least not healthy and honest ones. So if you think you've found one, he's probably an impostor, a fake, or a clingy possessive emotional parasite. My suggestion to you is to stop wasting time and try another planet.

Monogamy clearly goes against who we were created to be as a human family. It is unnatural and inorganic to our existence. **It actually goes against the concept of unconditional love**. In other words, if you are requiring someone you claim to be in love with to be monogamous, when you know in your heart that they're not. You do not love that person unconditionally or otherwise. How could you truly love someone when you're requiring him or her to change the very core of who they are? Then you obviously do not love that person. What you love is an idea that's an illusion not a reality. So stop lying to yourself and everyone else...

Listen! **"It's not the person who's acting in accordance with him or her organic self that's sick, it's actually the people who're not willing to accept the realities and truths of that person that is"**. Think about it!

Monogamy is morally toxic to our happiness and makes us weaker and much easier to control. It reeks of selfishness and always leads to dishonesty. It divides us. Which is probably one of the reasons for its implementation. Actually this rings true within my spirit so I'll repeat it: "One of the reasons monogamy was probably implemented is to divide us, making us weaker and much easier to control. This is why it has not only been strongly advocated, but legally enforced within western society". Obviously!

In addition to that, it deceptively pits us against each other and causes disharmony. It actually places women in a constant state of competition against each other, as opposed to a higher and healthier state of unified sisterhood. It also gives them more reasons to be angry with men: Men who've simply been unable to live up to the misguided monogamous expectations of not only them, but our society. We are all fighting against each other out of pure ignorance and the children are paying the heaviest price as a result of it. So what's the solution?

The solution is: We as a society need to remove the stigmatization of plural or polygamous relationships; by allowing their practice to be an acceptable option similar to monogamy, both from a legal and moral standpoint. This will allow for much more honesty between the sexes. It will basically eliminate that plaguing barrier between us, giving us far less reasons to be angry at each other. It will give us all the freedom to be honest and open to choose how we truly want to live our lives, without the bullying tactics of Church and Government consistently hanging over our heads; Threatening us with their monogamous propaganda and ridiculously hypocritical laws.

Eventually, this would not only stop the epidemic deterioration of the western family but also strengthen it. This is the direction we must take. We really don't have much of a choice. If we don't, we will be beaten into submission. Similar to when a natural disaster hits and everyone is forced to put differences aside and come together harmoniously.

In the following paragraphs, I will give more in-depth explanations as to how and why we've gotten ourselves into this disastrous situation; and why we should do everything conceivably possible to get out of it.

Is Monogamy An Obsession?

Well the answer to this question is a clear and definitive Yes. Our obsession to make monogamy the only acceptable form of romantic union from a moral, legal and religious standpoint has literally made us psychotic. If we take the time to investigate couples who claim to be completely monogamous, we will find that one or both partners already has, or will eventually violate the agreement. Monogamy at best has only been able to be a short-term fulfillment. It simply has not been sustainable, especially for men. There's absolutely no question that men are totally incompatible with monogamy; and I can personally attest to that. We see it as the enemy. It's not who we are, it stifles us.

The raw truth is: If men who are supposedly in monogamous relationships were to freely express

themselves sexually without all the static, they would consistently be servicing multiple sexual partners on a weekly basis. Which is definitely more in harmony with their true nature and far healthier for them on basically every level. Which now leads me to ask the question: Why in God's name should anyone not do that which is innate to him or her, particularly when it makes them healthier and happier? And keep religion out of this, I said God not religion. Well I'm waiting. Anything! Wow, nothing at all! I guess not!

That's exactly my point. It's absolutely clear to me that our behavior in terms of this matter makes absolutely no good sense whatsoever.

Listen! In order for anyone to be at their best, they need to be in harmony with their organic self sexually and otherwise. And I am willing to debate this with any human being.

I know this is very difficult for some people to come to terms with, but it's the truth. Which means it cannot and should not be ignored for any reason. Let's face it! It takes two to tango, and both parties have been living in this fantasy world for far too long. We are literally being held hostage by our monogamous exploits. We simply cannot win in a world where monogamy is mandatory. It is a lie plain and simple. Sooner or later we'll simply have to pack up and leave, or be destroyed. That's a fact!

Tell Me Why?

Just think about it! From the beginning of time the world has consistently been ruled by the male species. And for all that time men have never been truly monogamous: Especially the ones in power. So why then is monogamy the law of the land in some western countries (such as the United States), where men have always been at the helm? Why would they put something in place they themselves have never been able to live up to? What's the purpose of it? Why has it been so strongly advocated and enforced? What good has come of it, as opposed to the negative effects it has been having on our families and our society? And finally, why do we continually pursue it when it has proven to be a monumental failure?

The truth is, we've been continuously bombarded with images of fantasy and fiction. These images have filled us with false hopes and unrealistic expectations. To put it in a nutshell, we have been systematically programmed into wishing on a star that's never going to materialize. We are being played for fools.

I've got another important question for you: How many couples do you know to have sustained a completely monogamous relationship until death parted them? Remember now! Murder doesn't count. Don't rush take your time! Ok time is up! You can't think of anyone can you? Exactly! If that doesn't give you pause then something has to be seriously wrong with you. Obviously!

You see! Once the family is broken, it starts a vicious chain reaction of negativity, ignorance and frustration: One that has been continuously recycling throughout time. Regardless of how you twist it, monogamy is social warfare, and it's destroying us at the core.

Let Nature Be Your Guide

According to various scientific studies, over 97% of all mammals are polygamous. With the male being the dominant figure in most cases. There's also growing evidence that extra curricular activity occurs with the remaining 3%. So it is very obvious whoever created this planet and us, clearly didn't think of monogamy as being a good idea. In fact they were almost completely against it. It's not even close. It's a blowout landslide in favor of polygamy.

*So let's face it, Our Creator or Creators are clearly and emphatically saying to us that polygamous type relationships are best. It is why the percentage is so high, there's no argument here. (**And please don't use that ridiculous argument that we're not animals; actually in some instances we are worst. We kill each*** *other for absolutely no good reason). So we need to stop with this insane nonsense. Just think about it, if monogamy were right for us it would have had a much higher success rate than it has. The results would have bared it out. But it hasn't, and we keep overlooking that fact. Results are there to tell us whether something is achieving its intended goal or not. So we simply cannot ignore results because we don't like them. We're supposed to use them, as a means of making an effective judgment. And we're not!*

Let's Just Keep It Real

Ladies, let me tell you! Any heterosexual man who claims his heart's desire is to be in a completely monogamous relationship with you for a lifetime is either naive, weak, or flat out lying. And in most cases it's the latter (even though he may truly love you). If you don't believe me just have him submit to a lie detector test, or spy on him when he believes you're not looking. Actually I have a better one: Give him a truth serum to drink. I guarantee you he will prove what I'm saying to be absolutely true once he starts spilling his guts. There's simply no way of getting around the fact that men are not monogamous. So all you hypocrites I'm calling you out...

Listen! **"You cannot compromise the truth. Once you do it's simply not the truth anymore". Don't get** *me wrong! There are a whole lot of men who may claim to be practicing monogamy, but that doesn't make them monogamous. Trust me, these men are secretly under duress. Most of them are actually frustrated and miserable. Metaphorically speaking they're living in closets they're dying to get out of. This usually affects them in very negative ways both physically and mentally. Eventually many become toxic and prematurely inadequate. To be honest, it makes them sick. Walking the streets like stiff neck robots whenever they're with their ladies, trying hard not to expose themselves: Smoking and drinking heavily in order to ease their frustrations. Listen! Once you're not in harmony with your true or organic self you're destined to get sick. Hence why we as a society are so socially dysfunctional.*

But seeing that we have proven ourselves to be incredibly stubborn, there's a whole lot more I have to say on this topic, so read on.

From A Practical Standpoint

So far in this chapter I've been asking a number of questions. Why? Because I truly believe the right questions often leads to the right answers. So with that here's another one for you: **Did you ever stop to figured out why the higher-ups are so adamantly opposed to plural relationships? After all what's the** *big deal, who is it hurting? But here's the real question: What is wrong with two adult women and one adult man honestly and openly coming together, to love and support each other as a family? Be honest! Is there anything wrong with it? Listen! The answer on every practical and non-religious or non-hypocritical level is an emphatic nothing. In fact this is clearly the most natural and healthiest of all romantic unions in my opinion. It's much more honest, sensible and less burdensome not to mention empowering. I truly believe we'll be much better off practically, especially in these hard economic times.*

Right now we're in the midst of a vicious economic downturn and need to come together in a more practical way: Particularly African Americans who've been hit the hardest and is suffering the most.

It's totally incomprehensible to me why the government in good conscience, would consider prosecuting anyone for being part of this most natural union. Again, what are they afraid of? Even if you disagree with me, you have to admit this restriction is deeply troubling. It definitely discredits our claim of being a free society. It's not even civilized. To be honest! It's senseless and downright unfair.

Let's Just Be Honest

Ladies, my beautiful ladies! If you listen to the lyrics of Mary J Blige's song "Mr. Wrong", it actually figures out your confusion to an extent. There seem to be a lot of truth in what she's saying. The lyrics are basically saying: Bad boys are no good, and good boys are no fun. And although the bad boy aka Mr. wrong breaks her heart so bad, she prefers to deal with him as opposed to the so-called good boy. So what I believe Mary is essentially saying, is that the good boy who appears to be monogamous does not turn her on. He bores her. She's more turned on by the one who isn't. The truth is ladies, most of you are not happy with your so-called monogamous men either: At least not nearly as much as you claim to be. It's more like an obsession that's not really doing the job and you're in denial about it. After a while you start loosing interest romantically. That's a fact!!!

You see! The problem is your nature won't allow you to love the so-called Mr. Right the way you're supposed to. Why? Because he's a fake, he's not real. For him to honestly be that way, he has to be broken. Like an ex-fighter who've been beaten into retirement, with his hunger and innate predatory prowess greatly diminished. Which makes him appear very dull and unexciting, particularly to you ladies: Void of all the things that attracted you to him in the first place.

*Ultimately he's likely to become useless and repulsive to you. Listen, you can't have it both ways. At some point you have to stop lying to yourself. This is the dilemma for most of you. Out or pure ignorance, you are consistently attempting to turn men into something you or anyone else doesn't like, Zombies! You might not be willing to admit it, but it is for precisely this reason Mr. Right frequently gets cheated on. And that ladies, is the **Raw Truth!***

Just to let you know that there's no hypocrisy here. Exactly what I'm telling you is what I've been telling my beautiful daughter, whom I love more than anything. Although I don't believe she's listening at this point. Like most of you, she is extremely stubborn and in denial!

Why Can't We Be Friends?

*I've had many conversations with women who confessed to being very unhappy and frustrated with their relationship status. But almost every time I attempted to speak truth to their problem they would get very offended and overly emotional. They simply were unable to handle the truth. They preferred to embrace the fantasy, the myth. Some women actually said to me in no uncertain terms that they preferred to be lied to. Their exact words were, **"I don't want to know if my man has another woman".** I have to tell* *you! When you could verbally say something like that and mean it, you have a very serious problem. You are not only in denial, but you are suffering from an emotionally illness. This type of jealousy filled illness is a very common symptom of monogamy.* **"Once the Truth can be so easily dismissed, regardless of the situation, unhappiness is assured".**

This plague is the major saboteur of most relationships. It is truly an epidemically sad situation. As a society we have an extremely harmful and toxic addiction to monogamy and we are resisting any type of rehabilitation. We simply refuse to even entertain the idea (particularly the ladies); it's crazy. What makes the situation even crazier and more saddening for the ladies is that they have absolutely no real solution to the problem. They are miserable!

I can't tell you how many times I've heard women say, "all men are dogs", as they continuously search to find one that's not. (If all men are dogs, shouldn't you ladies be trying to find men that are good dogs as opposed to men that are not? Obviously they don't exist)! Men have been dogs (polygamous) since the beginning of time. You would think by now it would've dawned on everyone, that maybe it's the way we're supposed to be and accept it.

"All men are bad" is how one lady actually put it. When I disagreed with her, she became very angry and

hastily walked off. I could still recall the look in her eyes. They were filled with anger and bitterness. It was very obvious to me that she had been severely traumatized. I was completely stunned by her reaction. I actually felt very sorry for her. Saying all men are bad is like saying all lions are bad due to their sexual nature. We seem to have this huge problem with understanding the importance of accepting Nature. In order for us to survive in this world, this is a problem we simply must overcome.

Hypothetically Speaking (Sort Of)

Ladies, Be honest! You know every time your man go out alone; you start wondering and worrying to some degree whether he's going to pursue or give in to the temptations of some irresistible woman, especially if he's rated top of the line grade A. After all, these women are out there like a virus: Those young, hungry, beautiful, sexy and sometimes sluttish women. They're just ready to take on your man. How could you blame them? Remember now, **by embracing monogamy you've actually agreed to be part of winner take all contests and your man attracts the very best of the competition**, seeing that he's top of the line grade A. Which means you're going to be relentlessly challenged by opponents who want to dethrone you. And being in a so-called marriage, only motivates some competitors to challenge you even more. Why?

Because it shows that you man has been able to go all the way and fully commit. So it's only a matter of time before one or more of your competitors penetrate his defenses and get the better of you. Maybe even dethrone you. You see, regardless of how much your man loves you; he will eventually crack under pressure and give in or feel stifled and sick with frustration if he doesn't. Why, because Nature dictates it. So slowly but surely as time passes, the pressure builds, and you become increasingly suspicious and paranoid. Your attempts to suppress it become futile. Eventually the situation gets overwhelming and you transform into a private investigator, aka a snoop. Continuously searching for anything to justify your suspicions. Now you start getting upset over little insignificant things. Jealousy and insecurity begin to show their big ugly heads. Ultimately you become unhappy and completely frustrated. You are now primed for the knockout. Like a boxer who had been pummeled throughout a long grueling fight, you are vulnerable; and all your opponents could clearly sense it as they begin closing in on your territory. You increasingly need reassurance. Consistently needing to know whether you're still desirable. So you approach the mirror on the wall and ask the big question: Am I the most beautiful of them all? And the mirror replies with an emphatic "No, not any more". As a result of all the stress of trying to hold on to your prized grade-A possession (that you're unwilling to share): Your once beautiful face with the attractive smile has now been transformed into a consistent frown of desperation and gloom. You are miserable!

I must tell you, **"Insecurity is a hungry beast that's impossible for anyone to satisfy. Not your man, not your friend, not your priest, not your psychiatrist, not even you can satisfy this beast with a bottomless pit for a stomach. The more it's fed is the more it desires. The only way to overcome Insecurity the beast is to kill it by drowning it with the spirit of inner love and truth. Inner love and truth then manifests inner beauty, which is not only ageless and timeless but powerfully illuminating to your entire existence".** But right now that's not happening. So you start thinking about giving in to the grade B dog that had been sniffing around. You know the one! The same guy who's been frequently complimenting you by telling you everything you've been longing to hear from your man, systematically fattening you for the kill. Like a vicious dog stalking a vulnerable kitten, he's just licking his chops and patiently waiting for the right opportunity to **pounce** on you.

But you being the classy woman that you are, you decide to hold off on that crazy idea and seek some counseling. Unfortunately the counseling isn't working. How could it? The counselor simply doesn't have the audacity to tell you the truth even if he knows it. He is limited to some form of clichéd monogamous solution.

What he really needs to tell you is that monogamy is a myth, and their need to be honesty and realism in your relationship so that betrayal can be avoided. He needs to tell you that you're in love with the illusion of marriage and not the reality of it or the man. But he doesn't do that. So eventually you give in to that grade B dog.

*With that, your man starts noticing the change in your behavior after you've been relentlessly **pounced** on. So he gets even more frustrated and goes on a feeding frenzy. After all! He got tired of being on that strict and unnatural diet; which is now compounded by your persistent distrust and negativity. At this point, even a grade F feline has a chance at a one-night stand with him. Hey! His nature finally kicks in, and he's far less picky sexually than you are. Now your romantic relationship is done and the real battle begins. That's when you vindictively decide to inform him of that grade B dog you had allowed to viciously pounce on you in order to hurt him. With that he may get violent. Hey! He still thinks he owns you and you him. If you have a family it's now in turmoil. Unfortunately, this is the scenario that has been consistently reoccurring within our society on a daily basis, and it's non-discriminatingly vicious!*

United We Stand, Divided We Fall

Even the most successful and beautiful people in the world can't sustain a lasting monogamous relationship. It is said that the height of insanity is when you do exactly the same thing over and over again without success. Which is exactly what we keep doing expecting a different result.

"Listen ladies, you are the backbone of all societies, when you're divided, the people are divided and significantly weaker. You actually run the show. You really do. You are the nurturer of all humanity. The divine unification of God, man and yourself takes place and ultimately materializes within you. You are charged with bringing life into this world; you are the sacred vessel of the ultimate unification, which is humanity's life creating process. You simply must embrace this reality with all positivity and fullness. You are the key. The bottom line is, with unity there's power, real power! Without it, we will forever remain vulnerable to victimization and oppression".

So you could continue to pursue monogamy the myth that's rapidly destroying our families and us; or you could pursue an alternative that's much more unifying and consistent with reality. At least we owe it to ourselves to try, and we ought to have the freedom to do so. Which means the government restrictions on this most personal issue will have to be removed. But it can't happen without you ladies, we must lead this charge together. It's all about our freedom and our families. The bottom line is, we should be totally free to make our own decisions without any interference from the elected hypocrites.

Are We Really Free?

Are we really free in America? Well by now we should all know the answer to this one; I'm quite sure I've answered it earlier. But seeing that we've proven to be extremely stubborn, I'm going to expound on the topic some more. So the answer to the question is No. We're not free in America. Not nearly as free as we ought to be; and the fact that we may have a little more freedom than most other countries isn't enough to justify our appalling situation. So as far as the U.S Government's take on marriage and polygamy is concerned we're definitely not free. We literally have legislators deciding how **We the People** should live our lives, telling us who we should love and how many lovers we're allowed to simultaneously have. Are we children? Hey, I've got to ask! They surely treat us as if we are. It's unbelievable! We're so lucky to have these wise men deciding everything for us helpless kids (sarcastically speaking). But seriously! Just the thought of having to live my life according to what these guys decide is vexing to my spirit. It is totally *unfair. It clearly violates our freedom.* **They are supposed to be there to safeguard our freedoms, not take them away.** *On top of all that, there appears to be a high level of infidelity occurring in government and I'm quite sure it's not going to end anytime soon. These guys are hypocrites plain and simple. It's like them telling us not to eat chicken, while many of them happily and secretly devour it on a daily basis. They really don't have the moral, judicial or any kind of right to be telling us (consenting adults) how to live our personal lives. We shouldn't even be having this ridiculous conversation. Especially when we are paying their salaries. It's like paying someone to insult, degrade and abuse you. It's horridly sadistic. They seem to forget that they are there to serve us (We the People) and represent our interest, not interfere with our personal lives.*

Slavery Is Dead, Right!

Now that it's clear we have a long ways to go before we can consider ourselves as being truly free in America; I'll take it further by saying, the slavery business on planet earth is alive and booming. Oh! You didn't know? Well I must tell you! It's not only alive and booming, it's also much more sophisticated and deceptive than ever before. It has evolved and expanded to include all races and nationalities. So much so that approximately 98% of all Americans are economically enslaved and don't even know it. Sadly... That's only the half of it. We are also completely unaware that we are mired in social and emotional bondage; and monogamy is a major part of that bondage. As I mentioned earlier, we are being held hostage by it.

Under the strong influence of Church and Government aka (religiously wrapped brainwashing), we have been placing ourselves into monogamous boxes. Boxes that become legal when we choose to enter into Holy Matrimony: With the key word, or in this case, (weapon of deceptive control) being "Holy". You heard me! The word holy is being used, as a control weapon that deceives us into thinking our current system of marriage is sacred, and it's not...

Whenever we attempt to free ourselves from these restrictive matrimonial boxes, we get punished. Punished by means of merciless social whippings. Not only by society, but also by some of our brainwashed friends who supposedly love us and have our best interest at heart. Yeah right!

Two great examples of these types of whippings are golfer Tiger Woods and former President Bill Clinton.

President Clinton, who is one of our greatest presidents in recent memory, was actually impeached as a result of his perceived infidelity. He came very close to losing his presidency. Fortunately, he hung in there throughout all the nonsense, and his wife Hillary courageously stood by his side. Personally, I give her a lot of credit for not allowing the situation to overwhelm her. She never allowed it to destroy her relationship with her husband. Now that the smoke has cleared, Bill Clinton is now viewed as one of the most beloved politicians in America and around the world.

Well, what can I say about Tiger Woods, the destined to be greatest golfer of all time.

*In addition to being mercilessly whipped and ridiculed, he not only lost his wife; He also gave up a whole lot of cash along with a whole lot of ass in order to appease society's hypocrites. He was also blackmailed into entering a sex rehab program, or as I prefer to call it, **Neutering**. All this occurred when it was discovered he was having sexual relationships with other women besides his wife. Obviously it was something he chose to do that made him happy: The key words here being "Chose", and "Happy". As far as I know, that's what adults of a free society are supposed to be able to do. We are supposed to be free to choose whatever makes us happy, once we're not physically hurting or violating anyone's civil rights. Mind you! It would be great if we were allowed to be more honest and open about our actions. But unfortunately we haven't yet evolved to that level of wisdom and understanding. So Tiger was neutered! I* guess that's what we do to dogs these days; we neuter them. And according to our hypocritical society, Tiger was a very wild dog...

Just the mere sight of the slobbering hoards of robotic hypocrites lining up and unapologetically whipping these two men was utterly appalling. It was as though they forcefully raped these women. The hypocrisy of the two situations was disgustingly shameful. The media were like packs of wild frothing at the mouth hyenas, viciously ripping apart bloody carcasses. If it were at all possible, these two men would have been physically beaten and placed behind bars.

We have painted ourselves into such a corner when it pertains to monogamy, we can't even see past it. We can't even mention or talk about other alternatives, especially the P word.

If someone is brave and honest enough to even speak about, or openly practice polygamy. They could easily get chained up and put into an official box with steel bars. Also known as Prison!

So here we are, literally being forced to accept that we can only have one legal sex partner (openly); And If we decide to exercise our supposed (but illusionary) freedom and exceed our prescribed limitation, we are likely to be psychologically whipped and physically put into chains. It seems that we have no choice but to lie, *as opposed to being honest. I don't know about you, but this definitely seems like slavery to me. It's no wonder why we could never find true happiness. **In order to be truly happy, we need to be truly free; and we are definitely not!***

I'm Nothing Like You!

As I've mentioned earlier, men and women are vastly different emotionally; hence they cheat for completely different reasons. When my sisters cheat, it's usually from a negative place of dissatisfaction. Either they're not with the man they truly love, or if they are, he probably cheated on them and they're enacting revenge. Regardless of what it is, if my sisters are able to find that special man who they're truly in love with, one who's in harmony with their spirit; One who has the ability to make them laugh when he chooses and weaken their knees simply by looking at them, then it's quite possible for my sisters to be completely satisfied with that man. The hardest obstacle for them is overcoming their monogamous obsession and loving him for the good dog that he is.

On the other hand men are completely different. We could literally love you enough to die for you; and though everything might be perfect on the home front, sexually and otherwise, it's usually not enough to keep us from succumbing to the allure of other women.

Eventually, if we are exposed enough, we are going to give in. Sometimes the other woman doesn't even have to be all that alluring. The thing is, it almost never has anything to do with our partners. You see it's not really a competition with us. It's actually more about our nature and our erect penises... Hey don't knock it! An erect penis is not only the truth, but more importantly it's how we all got here.

One of the most interesting things I've noticed, is that when guys emotional feelings for the ladies get too excessive, we get stupid and out of balance. It tends to diminish our sexual prowess with them. Men need to have a healthy balance of emotion and physicality. I guess it is why it's so hard for us to just cuddle without having sex. Trust me ladies, you don't want a man who just wants to cuddle with you without having sex. Something is likely to be wrong with him. He has to be either sick or very close to death. Even if he's dead tired, once you start cuddling, he should want to have sex with you. If not, something is wrong. I suggest you call 911 or another woman to join you: Preferably the latter. Otherwise your relationship is probably on the verge of collapse.

We need to understand and respect that we're just not the same. We must learn to embrace our innate differences and appreciate our organic selves for romantic harmony to exist. In my opinion, it's the only way our relationships and family structure can survive for the long term.

Blind To The Fact

I view monogamy, as a "Tool of Deception and Oppression", a slick "Divide and Conquer" strategy. It is clearly the traitor in our midst, the enemy within. Monogamy is the Grim Reaper of the western family. The result is so shockingly deadly; it's like having a best friend who's been secretly sticking a knife in your back.

Just take a look at the African American community. According to recent statistics, approximately 72% of African American children live in a single parent home. The majority of these homes are fatherless with infidelity being the main culprit of the devastation; and I don't need any statistics to know this is true.

We are completely blind to the negative effects of monogamy and it's wreaking havoc on us. Any fighting expert would tell you, that the most devastating punch is the one that's unseen. That's usually the punch that knocks you out, cold! Well! Monogamy is knocking families out daily. As of now! Too many families that comprises of both parents are in the hospital's I.C.U on life support.

If we don't immediately rectify the problem, the

traditional black family, as we know it, is going to be the first to be rendered Extinct followed by the others.

Sadly... Too many of our children have already been victimized and mortally wounded by this devastating plague. Our insanely obsessive monogamous exploits have literally littered the romantic and social battlefields with corpses and injury-laden casualties; not to mention the added devastation and social dysfunction that has been specifically caused by post trauma and collateral damage. Simply put! This tragedy can only be described as being **Cultural Genocide**...

The Battle Of Religious Geniuses

Monogamy as we all know is stringently mandated by our western Judeo-Christian culture. In other words anyone who practices polygamy is negatively viewed as going against the word of God (a sinner). Therefore I'm forced to ask the question; how could this extreme view be right or even just?

How could polygamy, a practice that had been acceptable in the bible's old testament, be now viewed as unacceptable in the new? Assuming that both testaments are the word of God, how then could God the Creator of the universe who is supposed to be perfect in every way contradict himself like this? How could there even be a new testament? This simply doesn't add up. To accept it would be to accept that God is imperfect. It would imply that he had a change of heart, or was unable to foresee things. This is a blatant insult to our intelligence, not to mention God's existence. So forgive me! But I'm not buying it. If polygamy was acceptable for the highly blessed Solomon who reportedly had 700 wives and 300 concubines, then polygamy should be acceptable for everyone, forever!

So the question now is, where did the change occur and why?

Well! Allow me to answer that!

According to historical accounts on the early stages of Christianity, it is said that all ranks of the Catholic Church's clergy including the Popes, openly practiced polygamy, along with having concubines...

I want to be absolutely sure you heard me, so I'll repeat: The earlier practitioners of the Catholic Church including the Popes were blatant polygamists who also had concubines. Wow! This is very stunning!

It is also alleged that even Peter the first pope who is said to have been appointed by Jesus, was married with children. Which would clearly indicate that priestly sex was not only acceptable by Jesus, but also his heavenly father. Again, this is unbelievably *stunning! So if God and Jesus were cool with it, you've got to be wondering who had the audacity to change it? So let's find out!*

Well it seems as time went on, the Catholic Church started losing much of its property to the offspring of its polygamous clerics. Apparently back then the priesthood was more of a hereditary thing, and so was the church's property. This prompted changes in the church's doctrine, which led to the imposition of **monogamy** *and ultimately* **celibacy***.*

So contrary to popular belief, the practice of both celibacy and monogamy had absolutely nothing to do with God or Jesus Christ, it was all about the wealth, power and greed of the Catholic Church. This is when they began levying some reckless rhetoric and propaganda against polygamy and sex in order to justify the changes. Some of the church's clerics started labeling sex as sinful. There was a cleric by the name of St. Augustine (A.D. 354-430) who went as far as to state that an erect penis is a sign of man's insubordination.

This type of insane rhetoric is the root cause of our social chaos and sexual dilemma.

When you combine that with the Catholic Church's claim that women will forever be cursed as a result of Eve partaking of the Garden of Eden's forbidden fruit.

*You've entered the realm of insanity... **Think about it! Why would God eternally punish every woman as a result of Eve doing something he had to know she was going to do? After all, he is God; he's supposed to know everything. Right! Exactly!***

*I've got to tell you! This blatantly malicious demonization and obvious lying is the most socially damaging in the history of humanity. **"When you have the audacity to take the sexual unification of man and woman, which is the root of every human being's existence and demonize it. You have gone insanely mad. You have literally discredited all of humanity: Recklessly cursing the existence of you and everyone else. You have planted a wicked seed that has taken sex, which is in my opinion God's greatest gift to humanity, and made it a sin".***

*Without the erect penis of man and the vagina of woman to receive it, there would be no human beings walking around; including all those practitioners of lifetime celibacy. Actually without sex, there would be absolutely no intelligent life in existence. That's unless we can all be immaculately conceived. Like I said, it's pure insanity. **"When people have been brainwashed into disliking the essence of who they truly are, it's highly probable they would attempt to become something other than themselves. This ultimately leads to chaos and confusion. Making it extremely difficult, if not impossible for them to love themselves.***

Without self love, there is no love; and for far too long, we've consistently recycled this brainwashing".

When you really think about it, all of western culture's social behavior, which include monogamy, homosexuality and repressed sexuality, can be directly traced to St Augustine's and the Roman Catholic Church's demonization of the erect penis and womanhood. This is why their priest are required to be celibate, and we are all looked down upon as being born sinners: Simply because the act of sex has been made unholy by the Catholic Church. I guess it was Satan (who in my opinion is a figment of the Catholic Church's imagination) that created sex and not God. Obviously!

They weren't kidding when they said, "All roads lead to Rome". The truth is, they actually do!

By the way! I've already used some variations of these statements in other chapters of this book. But as you can clearly see, I'm not reusing them to be redundant, I'm reusing them simply because they apply to the current topic.

A Weapon Of Control

In ancient times, the hierarchy apparently came up with a strategy that would get the people to do and believe whatever they wanted them to; by convincing *them it was the word of God. As I mentioned earlier in the chapter The Art of Deception, they had discovered the most powerful and efficient control weapon in the history of humanity: A religious rubber stamp that was maliciously and deceitfully attributed to God's name every time it was used.*

They consistently used this rubber stamp with reckless abandonment to deceive and control the people without encountering much resistance from them, if any at all. Practically every war in history was started in the name of God and Religion. Even our system of marriage is stamped with this rubber stamp. It is why I said earlier, the word holy in holy matrimony is used more as a weapon of deceptive control

Listen! Only the couple involved in the relationship can make the bond real in the eyes of God, by personally and honestly committing to each other organically. No ceremony or priest can do that. It's just another part of the system of control. If the relationship isn't solid before the ceremony, it's likely to be much worst afterwards. That's unless the couple in question somehow gets enlightened of reality as in reading this book. When you really think about it, what did men and women do prior to the implementation of our marriage system? Exactly! I rest my case.

Who Do You Believe In?

*People! I've got another important question for you. Why do you think that it's possible for an eighty-year-old man to impregnate a much younger woman? Could anyone answer that one? You know what, don't even bother. Listen! We can't say we believe in God, and when God makes things very clear we consistently deny it. It's either we believe in God, or we don't. Even if we don't, the answer is still very clear. **Men have the innate ability to impregnate women until they die. So even when their wives can't have any more children, they can, with much younger women: Obviously! This clearly and unequivocally discredits the belief that we're supposed to be lifelong monogamous mates**. I truly believe that Nature, which is God's divine plan, is the way it is for specific reasons, and we should always try to embrace it without exception...*

Check this out! My grandfather was seventy-eight years old when he fathered my father. He also fathered my father's two younger brothers, with each of the three of them being two years apart. I have to tell you! My father and my uncles were literally super men. For instance, my father who's also 78 years old, is able to do 45 straight pull-ups on a pull-up bar. He's actually very close to doing a complete one-arm pull-up. A feat very few men on the planet of any age can accomplish (So I'm pretty sure he could still contribute to some baby making). One of my uncles was literally the greatest Steel drum pioneer to have ever walked this planet. In fact, all my uncles were great. So my grandfather was able to do his thing, and do it well enough to have contributed to the creation of such greatness. Case closed!

It's Time To Move!

Honestly! I see an expansion of the freedom movement, one that will include the people's freedom to have plural relationships. Seeing that gay rights and the marijuana restrictions are beginning to crumble. It only makes sense that plural relationships be also included, it's long overdue. The time has come for the people to have complete freedom. According to Martin Luther King Jr, it's time to Let Freedom Reign!

In terms of monogamy and polygamy, we definitely need to have an open and honest conversation. We need to think in terms of We, as opposed to I and Me. I personally feel that it really does take a village to raise a child, and as we all know the children are clearly suffering.

I also believe that monogamy leads to an increase in women choosing to have abortions. Without a unified or communal family structure abortion becomes a much more viable option, particularly when single women get pregnant. *So instead of restricting women from having abortions, we need to embrace a culture where women won't feel the need to have abortions. What I find ironic is that some of the more religiously extreme and fanatic advocates of monogamy are the people most opposed to abortions. Not realizing that it's their monogamous beliefs that may be causing a greater need for abortions.*

Hey Man, Tell The Truth!

*Monogamy turns men into liars. We agree to it only because we know it's what the ladies require. So in order to avoid the risk of losing them, we lie not only to them, but also ourselves: Thinking that we can successfully sustain a long-term monogamous relationship and be happy. My advice to my brothers is to tell the truth before you get intimate with that woman. Tell it as soon as you can: But definitely before sex. I know it's hard, but trust me, you will be better off in the long run. I won't lie! You may lose some potential lovers, but the ladies that stick around would be the ones that genuinely have more interest in you. They would also be the ones that respect your honesty; which in my opinion make for a much better situation. So we really need to stop with the lies and the hypocrisy. **Maybe if we all tell the truth, the ladies would start accepting us for who we are.***

Brothers Know Your Self and Your Health

My brothers you've got to know yourself. The effects that monogamy has on us who embrace it can be devastating, and even deadly. It's not organic to us. I truly believe that monogamy often leads to premature erectile dysfunction, impotency and prostate problems in men, even cancer. It limits our love making ability. We eventually become bored and disinterested or clingy and possessive. Which leads to our women also becoming disinterested. This could get guys cheated on really fast. I can personally attest to that.

In my entire romantic life, the only women that were a threat to cheat on me or who had actually cheated on me were the ones I had tried my hardest to please; by attempting to satisfy their monogamous expectations. Ironically! In all my plural relationships, I never at anytime felt the threat of being cheated on, not even remotely; And these women were just as beautiful as the ones I had placed on that unnatural pedestal. Figure that out!

Regardless of how beautiful our women are, for men to avoid complacency and sexual lifelessness, we need variety to keep us virile and stimulate us in a more regular and natural way. Especially when we get older. Unlike the ladies, we can't fake it, we need to get it up, and variety makes it more of a possibility without having to use a dangerous blue pill. The penis is a muscle just like any other, it needs constant stimulation and exercise to stay in shape and keep the rest of our body in shape. According to many doctors, there's growing evidence that more sex equals a healthier and longer life. Less sex leads to poor health and a shorter life.

Hey guys if you're not on top of your game, before you know it your woman who was so crazy about you in the beginning, might be telling you she loves you but she's no longer in love with you (very confusing). Then shortly afterwards, she may be asking you for a separation or even a divorce.

You have now lost your luster and your woman; without a clue as to exactly why it happened. According to Mary J Blige, you probably became Mr. Right. Trust me! It's the enemy within, and it could happen to the best of us. When it happened to me, Oops! That slipped out. In any event it did, and though I completely loved the woman in question, it made no difference.

The Truth Liberates Us

After I separated from the aforementioned woman in question, I made a conscious decision to abandon my monogamous exploits and be totally open and honest with my ladies. *Without exaggeration, it turned out to be one of the greatest decisions I've ever made in my entire life. The result was like: Wow! Jackpot! Fireworks! Bells ringing. I could fly. My whole world opened up and I became free, powerful and unburdened. Like a freed lion that had been caged all its life, I was finally liberated. I found truth. It felt not only good, but also right. I was growing spiritually. I became a greater man and superior lover. My women were reaping the spiritual and sexual benefits of a man in harmony with his true self. I was glowing so much, that even other normally competitive and envious men were amazingly drawn to my liberated aura. They would do and say things out of character. I remember this one guy I had met for the first time asking his niece if I were her man; but before she answered he immediately said to her if I was, she had a very good man. I also remember another guy telling his cousin the same thing shortly after meeting me for the first time. It was truly astonishing to see what a positive impact I had on those people. It was real!*

Let's Talk About Sex

Sexually! I don't mean to be boastful or too explicit, but it's absolutely necessary for me to reveal some sexual details in order to make my case for and against the topic at hand; Due to the fact that sex tend to be the biggest argument opponents have against plural relationships.

So here goes! In most, if not all instances during my plural relationships, my ladies seem to be enjoying as good or better sex than they previously had in their so called monogamous relationships. The sexual quality was great and orgasm count greater in most if not all instances. At least that's consistently the feedback I got. So based on their reaction and the fact I had to check their pulse every time we made love, (a very mild exaggeration). I see no reason to disbelieve them. One thing I know for sure, everyone was having great sex.

*In a couple of instances, my ladies went to levels of gratification we both never thought was possible (no exaggeration). It simply blew my mind. It was extraordinary, and I'm talking about grown experienced women. So the question now is why? Why were these women consistently having great sex in a situation that was supposed to be terrible for them? Obviously something had to be right for such positive results to consistently occur. Again, we have to look at the results in order to make an effective judgment. And I'll have to say, that an orgasm without question is the **Truth**, and a heavenly one at that! Especially when they are occurring multiple times...*

Psychologically! I've realized that the existence of an additional woman or women in the romantic equation, seem to enhance the appeal of the man in question. It makes him more desirable; which seem to enable some ladies to reach a higher level of passion and ecstasy. What can I say! Maybe it's because a female's orgasm starts in her brain, and the effect of a man in his true element is naturally more stimulating to her. So regardless of the reason! For me the sex was much greater than it was in my fake monogamous days, and it seemed even greater for the ladies. This is indisputable!

In My Not So Humble Opinion

In my opinion, other than the unproven and unjustified sexual taboos and population growth issues, polygamous relationships are far more advantageous. From a financial and general support standpoint it's clearly a more unified approach. This ultimately makes the family unit stronger. Personally! The experiences I had with multiple women were definitely better and less toxic on every level. There was more positive interaction between the ladies and far less disagreements than with my monogamous exploits. Everything was out in the open! Contrary to popular belief the ladies never attempted to kill themselves, each other or me. Imagine that!

In any event, the experiences were certainly great while they lasted.

Ok! You're thinking if the relationships were so great, why didn't they last. Well! Unlike most monogamous couples that often stayed in toxic relationships that usually resulted in them cheating on each other or worse. My ladies were free to exit the relationship at any time without having to deal with any needless drama and toxicity. So whenever they were unable to overcome their (happily ever after) monogamous fantasies, we cordially went our separate ways; which is cool, (Although I truly believe that they regretted leaving). At the end of the day we don't own each other, which means we should always be free to do what pleases us. It's all about freedom and honesty. Hey! It can be incredibly difficult to change particularly when you've had the same belief all your life; And almost everyone you've ever known and trusted, passionately promotes that same belief. The pressure can be overwhelming!

What's really messed up, is that many of the promoters of those flawed beliefs are either alone and miserable or frustrated and unhappy with their current romantic situation. It is as though they need to ensure that everyone be as miserable as they are.

I've got to say the ladies and I for the most part still remained friends, in lieu of their departure. The truth is! There's absolutely no doubt in my mind that being involved in plural relationships took me to the mountaintop, and seem to have taken my ladies to a much higher and healthier place also. Although I'm quite sure they didn't realize it at the time.

The Grand Finale

In my final analysis, I firmly believe we as a society urgently need to discover what's truly healthier for us and make a conscious decision to follow that path while learning to acquire a taste for it. At the end of the day we desperately need to find and embrace truth. Without it, it's impossible to attain Inner peace. Metaphorically speaking we should look at the situation this way: Monogamy is representative of the unhealthy foods we love to eat that's slowly but surely killing us; As opposed to polygamy, which is the organic foods we need to eat in order to be healthy and strong. We simply need to holistically modify our social taste buds so that we can acquire a taste for it. Hey! No pain, no gain.

To be honest, we need to take the same approach with many things in our society we're addicted to that are clearly harmful to our wellness: Not just monogamy.

Now there are many doubters who will say my views are insane. All I have to say to that is; **"a sane person will often appear insane in an insane world"**. At the end of the day I truly believe if my doubters are able to *have an open mind, in time they'll eventually come to agree with me.*

In closing, I wish everyone including the doubters, all the best in their quest for love and happiness. I sincerely hope I was able to shed some light and be of some help.

To my past lovers, I wish you all nothing but the best. I want every one of you to know that I am very thankful and grateful for what we've had. I've had absolutely no regrets. None whatsoever...

I sincerely hope you're all able to find true love and happiness. The bottom line is we are all attempting to figure out this tricky and confusing thing called life. We all want to find that elusive holy grail. So in closing, I will leave you with this:

"*O*nce we're able to continuously live with love and firmly embrace truth whenever and wherever we find it. Then the Holy Grail is firmly within our grasp".

Fourteen

The Third Eye

(I See You)

*C*lose *your eyes and you'll see the truth. Be silent in meditation and you will not only hear and see, but you will also know as in knowing, or as in knowledge. So what is the third eye? The third eye is our spiritual vision; otherwise referred to as our heightened intuition. It is our ability to read the entire book by its cover, or even without physically seeing it at all. It is the psychic capability we all possess. When developed, it makes us a whole lot more powerful. It gives us superior insight. In a sense, it's our spiritual telescope. It is what we should all be guided by. It makes us wise as in Wisdom.*

An undeveloped third eye is a clear indication we're not tapped into our Inner God. It makes us much more vulnerable and susceptible to adversity and even death. It means we are literally blind not just to pending dangers, but also favorable possibilities that may be on the horizon. It makes us more liable to make bad decisions. It also makes us much easier to be lied to. So it is extremely crucial that our third eye be developed. Once we keep working on awakening our Inner God the development of our third eye will increase. It is a process of continuous growth.

I'm not saying a person with a developed third eye is not going to make mistakes. They are; just not nearly as much as a person without one. Sometimes out of sheer need and desperation we may overlook what our third eye is subtly showing us. For example you may be desperately short on cash and as a result, go with an opportunity you may have sensed to be shaky and end up regretting it. The same thing could happen with a sexual situation, so you need to be careful. But at the end of the day, once you are a person that's conscious and living righteously; there's usually an important lesson or positive outcome behind any perceived mistake you might make: More often that not, you will be stronger and much better off in the long run as a result of it.

The third eye is usually at its best after a full night of sleep just prior to awakening. It is why the best practice is to sleep on it before making important decisions. So whenever you're not sure, always remember to close your eyes, look within and wait for the answer. Know that all answers lie within, particularly the best ones.

Fifteen

Wisdom Rules

(Wise Man = Simple Man)

*W*isdom is Supreme! If Knowledge and Understanding is power: And in my opinion they truly are. Then Wisdom stands firmly at the side of the throne Love sits on, with Truth proudly standing on the opposite side. Wisdom enables us to find the simplest solutions to some of the most complex problems. It simplifies our existence. Wherever you find true wisdom you're sure to find Spirituality and Truth. Wisdom is priceless. A truly wise individual can profoundly change a person's life for the better in the matter of a few minutes, or with only a few words. There are many unsuccessful people who are simply a few minutes of wisdom away from knowing how to fulfill their dreams.

I distinctly recall an incident with a friend of mine who at the time couldn't figure out why he kept getting negative reactions from almost everyone he dealt with.

*To his amazement, I was able to figure out the root of his problem and set him on a better and more positive path in a couple of minutes. There's absolute no reason not to embrace wisdom. I say this because when it comes to Religion, we seem to throw wisdom completely out the window: Hence why we're so confused and misguided. So I will reiterate! Seeing that we often overlook the essence and fullness of things due to our social hardwiring: **"There's absolute no reason not to embrace Wisdom, none whatsoever! Especially when it pertains to Religion".***

*In order to have any chance of acquiring Wisdom there are some things we must do. We definitely need to have honesty. We must relentlessly and passionately seek truth, firmly embracing it whenever and wherever we find it. But the most important thing we need to do is tap into our spirit. **Wisdom is a highly spiritual thing and our spirit is the greatest truth finder and lie detector in existence.** So once we develop our Inner God and tap into it, we should have all the wisdom we need. Wisdom frequently goes beyond the knowledge at hand. A truly wise individual is one that uses the knowledge at hand more effectively in order to create higher intelligence. Ultimately higher intelligence is what leads to the best solutions.*

So to sum it up! We must all awaken our Inner God and allow the wisdom that emanates from it to guide us. Then we'll all be able to say that we are truly wise and

Wisdom does Rule!

Sixteen

The True Christ

(Christ walks, Jesus never did)

*T*he story of Jesus is by far the most important and compelling story in the history of humanity. According to Christians, Jesus was undoubtedly the greatest man that ever lived. It is believed by many that he was actually God in human form. Even the demarcation of time is based on his life and death. It is said that he was immaculately conceived by God himself and born of the Virgin Mary, (which I find very confusing to say the least. It implies that he conceived himself. Which impels me to ask the question: **Why?**). Anyway, let's continue! According to his followers, he has performed countless miracles: Such as walking on water, changing water into wine, making the blind see and bringing the dead back to life just to name some. He is said to be the truth, the way and the life, and also the divine savior of all of humanity. Christians believe that no one gets salvation unless Jesus is acknowledged as the one and only Savior.

In lieu of the awesome power and ability he allegedly possessed, a gang of mere mortals with evil and wicked intentions was also alleged to have brutally beaten and tortured him before crucifying him. Which resulted in him being mercilessly nailed to a wooden cross, where he ultimately took his last breath.

Many Christians believe that one day he will return. But based on their perceptions of his identity, so far all predictions of his return have proven to be false.

As a Christian I totally believed the story of Jesus to be true. I believed it because I was raised to, and everyone around me seemed to have believed it too. So as a youth growing up I never dared to question it. To do so would be to risk being crucified. A risk that's just as real and present even today; Which in itself is contradictory and highly controlling when you think about it. (If Jesus was who they say he was, why are we literally being forced to accept him? Obviously this goes against what he stood for). According to Martin Luther King Jr, we should "Let freedom reign": Just some food for thought.

In any event, as I started to grow as a man and more importantly as a spiritual being, I began having some very profound revelations that helped to open up my consciousness. The more I developed on a spiritual level is the more questionable the story of Jesus became.

It eventually awakened in me the realization that if we are going to invest our entire lives into anyone or anything especially if we believe our salvation depends on it: We must never hesitate to fully and relentlessly question it before totally committing ourselves. As a result, if our questions are not satisfactorily answered, then to totally commit ourselves is likely to be a very disappointing and non fulfilling investment; Which is why I've come to the stunning conclusion that the story of Jesus is a deviously concocted misrepresentation: One that's being used as a highly effective control mechanism, in order for us to be more tolerant and accepting of the relentless abuse and oppression we've long been subjected to. Everything within my spirit tells me the original story has been severely altered to such a degree, that it has been transformed from truth to sensationalized fiction. In other words, Jesus represents a highly sensationalized reenactment of a True Christ. His story simply put, is a lie...

Ironically as a child growing up in Trinidad, when you tell lies, the other children would say you're telling stories. So based to the children of Trinidad logic, I'll have to say, **"Jesus' story is a complete defiance of the truth, it insults not only our intelligence but basic common sense itself".** The story consist of way too many contradictions. It has left us without any trace of tangible evidence or proof of accomplishments in *order for us to authenticate its validity. The story's acceptance is totally based on belief and it shouldn't have to be if it was true. What further serves to exacerbate my suspicions; is the fact that the final editors of the story have had an unquestionably long and checkered past.*

They have undoubtedly committed a long list of unpunished crimes against humanity. They have proven to be untrustworthy and sadistically wicked. For us to believe they actually told the truth would be insanely foolish on our part.

These people possessed the most distinguished resume in terms of evil and warfare. They were and still are the masters of deception, greed, control and murder. They were the perpetrators of slavery and colonialism. They have forever been owners and users of weapons of mass destruction. I'm talking about the powers that be, the true hierarchy, which are the viciously greedy and underhanded money moguls that has always owned all the politicians and religious leaders. I'm talking about the most successful propaganda pushers in the history of humanity. I say pushers because their propaganda is used as an addictive drug.

These pushers have been pedaling some highly addictive forms of propaganda in the name of fantasy, fiction and blind hope. These forms of propaganda have allowed the hierarchy to stay in power, and deceptively control the minds and actions of the people for hundreds of years.

I have to tell you! Crack cocaine has nothing on these highly addictive forms of propaganda. They are so powerful and potent; almost the entire world is hooked on them. They have been effectively used to sell the masses on Religion with Jesus as its star player.

The fact that these propaganda pushers are the true authors of our religious and social doctrine is extremely troubling. As a result of us believing all the lies that were told to us by these extremely dubious characters is the prime reason for our dysfunction. With the huge amounts of deception we've been subjected to, how could we not be dysfunctional? It is why our quest for peace and happiness has been a monumental failure. Now I am very sure there are many in high places that knows what I'm saying is true. Unfortunately they are terribly afraid of the devastation that can occur if these truths are brought to light. But karma dictates that all truth will eventually come to light, and I'll have to say, that day is now upon us.

Listen! Common sense should tell us that much of the history and the stories that were told to us could never be true. We should know that the hierarchy's guilt simply wouldn't allow them to reveal the whole

truth. We should know that's how our system has literally been functioning for its entire history. As I said earlier, to totally believe the Jesus story without questioning it would be completely insane and foolish on our part.

The bottom line is, if we are to succeed in our quest for Inner Peace we need to embrace Truth, the whole truth and nothing but the truth. Thus far! What we've been embracing is far from it.

Once we're able to embrace the truth, then it's all about Love. For us to overcome the demons and the brainwashing that has prevented us from loving each other and ourselves, we need both spiritual and psychological surgery followed by some rehab for empowerment purposes.

Well! This chapter is a major part of that surgery and rehabilitation, so let's get started.

Oh! You taught we had already started? Actually that was just my way of preparing you. To abruptly expose you to the forthcoming information without some preparation: Might have been too extreme for some of you to handle. So I had to minimize the pain. Though it's still going to hurt to a lesser degree, the gain will by far outweigh the pain. In the end I guarantee you will greatly benefit from it. This information I'm about to bestow upon you is major, not *only will it liberate you from your demons and shackles, it will empower you! So let's get started.*

The story of Jesus I must admit is positive in some aspects. It's very hard to deny that and I won't. Its message of love, compassion and selflessness is greatly needed; it can be useful and beneficial in many ways. But there are some very important questions we all need to ask ourselves: Like who's benefiting the most from this sensational story, why are they benefiting, and at what price? I've got to say the answer is clearly the perpetrators of war and greed: The masters of deception and trickery. They benefit the most from it by a wide margin at our expense. Why? Well as I stated earlier, it is used as a weapon of control and deception among other things...

Think about it! Why would anyone of such devious and dubious character awaken us to anything that's empowering or helpful to us? Coming from that source, how could it ever be about our welfare when they themselves are not adhering to the same teachings and doctrine? It makes absolutely no sense whatsoever, so we seriously need to think about that.

Another deceptively negative belief and practice that can be attributed to Jesus is the implementation and justification of monogamy; which we now know stigmatizes our true sexuality, and is the seed of our epidemic social chaos. The truth is, in many ways we've been unknowingly supporting a very misleading and destructive agenda. One that has divided us and allowed evil, greed, poverty, oppression and hate to flourish; one that could lead us to the most brutal and devastating outcome in history, our destruction!

Listen! You cannot represent love, and at the same time be the bedrock for evil and hate. It simply cannot work that way. You've got to be for one or the other. According to the lyrics of a popular reggae song, "Love and hate could never be friends". Which is true they can't!

In the case of Jesus, his followers have committed some of the most egregious crimes in history and in large amounts. From the Popes and their undercover bosses to their subordinates and many of their followers: They are all guilty of a great many crimes. You name it and they've done it or sanctioned it, from slavery, colonialism and genocide to rape and pedophilia... I know some of you are going to say, "Jesus didn't do these crimes". Again, my answer to that is if he is who he's heralded to be, why can't he control his followers? Where is his power? What's the purpose of him? How good are his teachings if it has never ended suffering and brought peace to this world? How real is it, and how real is he? Honestly, I don't believe he's real at all, that's why throughout this chapter I've purposely left out the name Christ whenever I mentioned Jesus. I'm saying Jesus and

Christ are two separate individuals; they're not the same. One is real and the other is not. So we need to get to know the real Christ, the True Christ, so read on...

At this point you're either very angry if you're staunchly Christian, or your curiosity is spiking through the roof whether you are or not. In any event there's really nothing to be angry or fearful about. If you're not buying what I'm selling you could simply hold on to your current beliefs. So take a deep breath and let's continue on...

Right now I would assume there's a large light bulb on in your head as a result of your elevated curiosity and suspicions. If that's the case, it's good. You are now beginning to challenge everything with a more impassioned intensity including what I'm saying. Which is exactly what you need to do. And if and when you do, I'm extremely confident you will come to the inevitable conclusion that you've continuously and blatantly been lied to, and what I'm saying to you is very much closer to the truth.

Ultimately this will change you for the better. ***For unless you've truly found peace, you need to replace that which after 2000 years of relentless promoting has failed to bring you peace. It's that simple...***

The truth is, the underlying subliminal message of

Jesus is deceptively destructive and debilitating. It totally goes against the essence of who we are. In addition, it limits our growth and prevents us from reaching our highest potential. It weakens us! It also encourages us to give all the credit to a fictional character that couldn't have anything whatsoever to do with our successes. How many times have you seen hard working celebrities and athletes stand up and give thanks to their lord and savior Jesus Christ for doing absolutely nothing? Some even said it was all Jesus and had nothing to do with them. That's just crazy! I got to tell you, the brainwashing is deep!

Listen! The power that abides within us deserves most if not all the credit for what we do. I'm talking about an eternal power that cannot be crucified, Our Inner God.

We all need to wake up and understand that when we tap into our Inner God and trust in it by believing in our selves, once we work hard and never give up we will succeed. It's all within us. It has absolutely nothing to do with Jesus. If it did then there would be no need for hard work. We would all be able to persevere simply by accepting Jesus. Which I'll have to say is just not true!

With that said, the very elaborate story of Santa Claus comes to mind. I see a direct correlation between the story of Santa Claus and the story of Jesus.

The True Christ

In some aspects the story of Santa Claus appears to be good on the surface, but its true intent is deceptively bad; and as we all know the story of Santa Claus is completely made up. That's the trickery of these stories, there's always a hidden agenda. They are specifically created to subliminally manipulate, weaken and brainwash us, as you will soon discover if you haven't already done so.

As a child growing up in Trinidad, I distinctly remember writing to Santa Claus and asking him for a model car for Christmas, one that I could sit in and pedal. Well he eventually wrote me back stating that he couldn't get me the car but had something really nice for me instead (at least that's what I thought). I'm not sure at that time what I got, but I remember being a little disappointed, I really wanted that car. I was totally unaware that my extremely hard working parents had to struggle and sacrifice even harder, simply to get my siblings and I gifts for Christmas. So there I was an innocent child, living on an island that has never seen winter nor snow, depending on this chubby long bearded white guy from the north pole to fulfill all my Christmas desires. So instead of giving the credit to my beloved parents, I gave it all to Santa Claus (which is very similar to when we give all the credit to Jesus for doing absolutely nothing).

I don't believe I need to tell you how psychologically damaging these sorts of things are. The negative racial

Closer To Truth   159   Closer To Love

and cultural affect it had on us was unbelievably huge. It is clear that these seemingly harmless and sensational stories were actually very sophisticated weapons of social warfare and brainwashing. In fact, there was a whole lot of racially tainted brainwashing going on in Trinidad back in those days.

I distinctly remember almost every home having a picture of Jesus with the sacred heart and also one of him with his disciples at the last supper hanging on its walls. Naturally he was portrayed as being white with blue eyes. Which historically is highly questionable and laughable to say the least; and though most Trinidadians were mostly of African and East Indian descent, you couldn't dare question his features.

Then there was the picture of St Michael the so called archangel with the sword in his hand; Getting ready to slay the black devil with horns. Again, St Michael was white. He had to be! Obviously! Isn't that what all angels are (sarcastically speaking). These pictures were viewed as symbols of protection against evil, which means they were prominently displayed on the walls of virtually every home, usually over the doors.

I've got to tell you, having these images burnt into your psyche was extremely damaging, especially to a perceptive child like myself. I remember growing up with an extremely debilitating case of insecurity. I simply hated being dark skinned. All you had to do was call me anything with black or dark in front of it and I would be completely devastated. It was very bad. As handsome, peaceful and talented as I was, I hated myself. To be honest, I didn't know of anyone back in those days who was truly proud to be black. How could they? Black was not only ugly and evil but inferior, and the pictures of St Michael and Jesus reminded us of that perceived fact every day.

I also remember taking our toy guns and playing cowboys and Indians. Obviously no one wanted to be an Indian. Playing an Indian was like a punishment. Everyone wanted to be the good white cowboy, so they could get to kill the bad Indians. Let's not even talk about Tarzan king of the African jungle. Every male child in Trinidad was Tarzan, and we could all duplicate the tribal call he was so famous for in the movies. Astonishingly, this type of racially demeaning thinking was completely normal back in those days, and many people are still unknowingly suffering the affects of it.

Now! I don't want you to take this as some type of racial crusade I'm on. That's not what I'm about, and it's definitely not what this book is about. This is about exposing a strategy and culture of deception that has been implemented by some very selfish, greedy and downright wicked people. This is about exposing the root cause of humanity's painful dysfunction, by revealing the truth through the spiritual eye of an Anointed Warrior.

So before I go any further in discussing this Jesus story, I must warn you: **There are some scare tactics and negative labeling that have been commonly used to demonize and discredit anyone such as myself who dare to challenge the status quo. These tactics and labels are primarily used to instill fear and dissuade us from questioning the lies and getting to the truth.**

I can assure you once this book is released, that's exactly what's going to happen. But I'm not allowing it to impede me from speaking truth, and you must not allow it to inhibit you from embracing it.

Listen! Fear blocks growth and is the number one killer of dreams and aspirations. It prevents us from elevating to our best self. *These masters of deception use labels such as Anti Christ, Socialist, Atheist, un-American and Muslim among others in derogatory ways to instill fear and distort the truth.*

A great example of this is when President Bush under the guidance of Dick Cheney, deceptively used the term "Weapons of mass destruction" as a scare tactic and excuse to invade Iraq in 2003. That invasion literally brought the world to its knees and resulted in the unnecessary deaths of over 4000 Americans and a mere couple hundred thousand Iraqis. A minor detail (sarcastically speaking) we don't hear enough about in the American media. Some reports have the total death toll at upwards of 600,000 as a result of this totally unnecessary ten-year war. Honestly, America and the rest of the world still haven't fully recovered from that unjustified war. In addition to the staggering death toll, this war has led to some countries seeking to attain or increase their nuclear weaponry. Let's face it! George Bush and Dick Cheney's senseless actions have rendered America untrustworthy: And although President Obama has thanklessly helped to somewhat reverse the negative sentiments towards the United States, he isn't going to be in office forever. So the fear is that another Dick Cheney could attain power sometime in the future and do the same thing. Hey! It's highly possible. So that's the dilemma this unnecessary war has caused.

Another fear tactic some rivals have been using against President Obama is their continuous attempts to paint him as an un-American socialist. As though socialism is the great evil of the world. Well the reason why I brought this up is to inform all the Christians that believe in Jesus; that based on his story, Jesus was undeniably the greatest socialist of all time, and he definitely wasn't American if anything at all...

So before I allow these masters of deception to negatively define me, I'm going to preempt that by telling you exactly who I am and what I represent.

I am, and have always considered myself to be a true and obedient child of God (The Creator of the universe). I have made a pledge to be an inspired warrior for love, peace, truth, freedom, justice and fairness. I intend to walk this road with unrelenting purpose for this lifetime and all eternity if possible. I stand for the liberation of all humanity not just some. I stand for the liberation of all those who have suffered at the hands of injustice, as well as those who have benefitted from it. We are all victims of ignorance. Without complete liberation there can be no peace. My weapon of choice like Martin Luther King Jr, Malcolm X, Bob Marley and other warriors who came before me is my voice, my message. I am a proud and true messenger of this time.

I stand for unity: One people, one purpose and one race, the human race. I am pro Christ but anti Jesus. The story of Jesus after two thousand years has failed to unite this planet. Instead it has turned out to be a great divider... The deception lies in the hope and promise that he (Jesus) will one day return. Well, that's not going to happen. And even if he miraculously returns, I seriously doubt anyone is going to recognize him. The truth is; if his story were indeed true, the world would have been harmoniously united in peace 2000 years ago.

*So let me reiterate, **Jesus is a purposely- orchestrated misrepresentation and sensationalized*** *version of a True Christ. A fictional character, a mythical interpretation and deliberate exaggeration. He is the main character in a sinister plot that was devised to inspire peasants to be more contented with their meager existence and accepting of the abuse and suffering they were being consistently subjected to at the hands of their oppressors; while their oppressors were basking in excessive luxury and riches.*

Contrary to the doctrine of Jesus, the hierarchy would never turn the other cheek although they required the peasants to do so. In fact their justice was swift and deadly to all dissenters of their enforced doctrine. This mindset still prevails in today's culture. The trick was and still is, if God could allow his only begotten son to be brutally beaten, abused and eventually crucified for all of humanity's sins as they claim, then surely the peasants (which now refers to us) had nothing to complain about. They simply had to suck it up and feel extremely thankful and blessed they were alive and not dead like so many of their unfortunate brothers and sisters; Including Jesus!

I don't know about you, but this obvious deception and trickery is extremely insulting to my intelligence and should be to yours. And (the dying for our sins part) was the best excuse they could come up with to justify why God would allow his only begotten son, oh excuse me! His self to die after being brutally tortured *and crucified. This begs me to ask the question, who are these people's God? Just recently, I heard a very prominent religious leader state that God is grieving for his loss, and no one challenged him on it. Honestly, I am very curious to find out who is these people's God. He sounds very weak and troubled to me. The God that I obediently adhere to has no worthy challengers, he never grieves, and he is jealous of no one. Frankly! You better not even think about crucifying him.*

Listen! If God wanted to forgive us for our sins, I seriously doubt he would've done it that way. **The idea that God allowed himself or even his only son for that matter, to be dragged through the streets tortured and then mercilessly crucified by The Wicked for any reason; is the craziest lie in the history of this Universe. But what's even crazier, is the almost one billion people who honestly believe this is true.** *"When I stop to think about how long we've been foolishly believing these lies, the tremendous sadness and disgust I feel go way beyond words". This is sickening!!!*

Even the New Testament appears to have been made up in order to legitimize this myth. Once you start telling lies you usually have to cover them up with additional lies. The New Testament clearly fits that bill.

Let's assume the Old Testament was completely true and legitimate, although I seriously doubt that it was.

But let's assume that it was for a minute. There are some things in the New Testament that clearly contradicts the old: Such as our stance on polygamy among other things. If the old were indeed legitimate, its core doctrine should never be changed, it should stand for all eternity. There should be no disagreements or contradictions to it. After all, it is supposed to be the word of The Almighty God who is perfect!

To be honest! There shouldn't even be a New Testament. But the fact that there is one, is again utterly ridiculous and insulting. It is clearly an insult to the power of The Creator. It suggests he is weak, unsure and imperfect. Listen! When God makes a statement, the impact of that statement is unquestionable and powerful like the Sun.

Actually, it's the Sun of God we really should be praising, not a human who is said to be his only son. The Sun is 93 million miles away and it sustains all life on Earth. It's so hot and blinding you can't even get much closer to it; and you definitely cannot crucify it. If the Sun dies, humanity and all life on Earth will be done. There is no human being who has ever lived that remotely compares to it on any level.

So again I've got to reiterate, Jesus has supposedly been dead for over 2000 years, and the world literally hasn't skipped a beat. So we really need to stop with this insulting madness. If the Jesus story were true, the results would've at least bared it out to some degree. Since his alleged death, the world has never been at peace. There has been no significant improvement or change that we could point to and say, *(Wow! That's why Jesus died; everything is good now. The world is at peace).* There has been no aha moment like that.

Since the beginning of time all of humanity has been relentlessly pursuing happiness, but very few if any, have actually been able to truly achieve it. So where's the benefit of Jesus? I don't see any benefit that get's anywhere close to the hype. Again! The idea that anyone died for our sins is simply ridiculous. With the millions of poor innocent children literally dying of starvation in Africa and around the world, how could we possibly think that; And these poor children haven't committed any sins whatsoever.

So let's all agree right now that no one died for our sins; At least not the sins of regular people. Jesus must have died only for the sins of the rich and powerful. They seem to be the only ones consistently and blatantly getting away with murder. On the other hand when regular people remotely break some ridiculous law we usually receive swift unforgiving injustice. Many followers of Christianity will have little to no forgiveness for me. And all I'm attempting to do is help make this world a better place by revealing my truth and elevating the spirit of love. But there seems to be a consistently relentless desire to silence anyone who challenges this corrupted system with truth. Why is that? And what are they afraid of? Honestly, we need to Stand Up!

Listen people, if God is dissatisfied with anyone, he could easily take care of the situation himself. He clearly doesn't need any help. So all who feel the need to do evil things in the name of God really need to stop. It's stupid, it's crazy and it's just wrong.

It's mind boggling how gullible we've been to allow this stuff to completely go over our heads like it has. I say we because as I stated earlier, I used to believe in this stuff. I was raised as a Catholic and followed Christianity for the greater part of my religious life. Fortunately I was able to evolved past the ignorance and confinement of Religion and into the limitless realm of Spirituality.

Not to be redundant, but I will like you to again ask yourself these revealing questions; **Do we need to be Christian, Jewish or Islamic in order for us to be compassionate and kind to each other? Do we? Do we need to be exclusive followers of Jesus, Mohammed or any prophet for that matter in order to be good, caring and selfless people? Should a dying Jewish man be any more grateful to another Jewish person for saving his life as opposed to a Palestinian person doing exactly the same for him? The answer** *to all the above questions should be a very clear and unequivocal no. The message here is that love and compassion is not exclusive to any specific religion, group or person. We simply need to do the right things as individuals. We need to overcome our obsession of being religious gang members and avoid taking part in these religious gang wars.*

This is where humanity needs to be. Unfortunately, when we say that Jesus or any prophet of a specific religion is the only way to salvation. We are actually saying that The Creator of us all is limited to that specific religion forsaking all others. We are saying that it really doesn't matter if an individual saves all of humanity with a great deed. Once he doesn't accept Jesus as his lord and savior, he will never know salvation. This blatantly shameless lie is what's separating us. It's what's keeping us at war with each other. It's literally destroying the world and any hopes of peace.

According to historical accounts, the sensationalizing and maybe even the orchestration of the Jesus story occurred at the Council of Nicaea, at the hands of the Roman Emperor Constantine during the fourth century, as I stated earlier in the chapter (Love Is My Religion). This is where Constantine basically dictated to the Catholic bishops what the Christian doctrine was going to be. So it was in fact more about satisfying a political leader's personal agenda than the truth. This is why the story will never stand or add up.

If we really think about it, there isn't any hard evidence of Jesus' existence, there's nothing he has personally written not even a note. He reportedly never had a wife or any children. So for us all to aspire to be like him and follow in his footsteps in that aspect would mean the end of humanity: Likewise the Pope, the Catholic Priests, the Nuns and all practitioners of lifetime celibacy. Unless we can all be immaculately conceived. Humanity will surely end. Even the heralding of the "Immaculate Conception" is suspicious and highly contradictive in my opinion. To me, it consciously and subconsciously stigmatizes the sexual union between man and woman that results in the creation of new life. It implies that this sexual process is flawed and not perfect. In doing so, it again questions the perfection of The Most High Creator who himself created this divine and wonderful process. Which should unquestionably verify its perfection. "This stigmatization of the sexual process is the root cause of humanity's sexual repression and emotional confusion. The truth is, our entire belief system is littered with too many undetected lies".

The bottom line is; the people who've decided that time should be distinguished by the life of Jesus; the ones who were responsible for the religious doctrine the masses have been made to follow, have never followed it themselves. Which should be a very clear indication that the story of Jesus isn't true.

With that, let's get into the real nitty-gritty of why the hierarchy decided that it was necessary to use the Jesus story to deceive us.

My feeling is that the reason the sensationalized story of Jesus was manufactured was because of race. I truly believe race was a major reason for the deception. *Everything in my spirit and even my intellect tells me that the original Christ figure or figures that were the basis for the Jesus story were probably Nubian. At best they were of the darker hue.*

It seems to me that the Roman colonialists took the story of a Christ figure or figures and used it to their advantage by changing the image to reflect their own image and likeness. If you really think about it, why would any oppressor promote the greatness of any person who is the same image and likeness of their victims, particularly back in those days? That's why Jesus' projected image never made sense. It's why we can't seem to find any hard evidence of his existence. There's hard evidence of far less important men who've lived long before they claimed Jesus did, while there's absolutely no evidence of the greatest man that ever walked the earth: A man that allegedly had twelve disciples and a slew of followers, not to mention a mother and stepfather. A man who supposedly knew exactly when he was going to die and whose existence is the basis for the measurement of time. I truly believe if any hard evidence does exist, it is purposely not being revealed. If it were to be revealed it would expose all the lies. Honestly! I don't know how anyone could choose to ignore these questions. If this were the court of law, the case would've been instantly thrown out for lack of evidence and plagiarism on the religious zealots' part. Well, I've got to tell you! This is a much higher court than any other in existence... This is humanity's court of Truth and Redemption. **The time has come for all Religions and all Churches to come clean. It's time for them to tell the truth, the whole truth and nothing but the truth. It's time to own up to and atone for all transgressions. It's time for Love and Truth to be fully embraced and harmoniously cover this Earth.**

So the question now is, what and who is The True Christ?

"The True Christ is one who's anointed with the spirit of The Most High Creator: A beautiful manifestation of all that's good and right within humanity. A Spiritual Warrior that exists at the highest level of human spirituality and consciousness. The True Christ is a mystical and magical representation of peace; who's filled with love and compassion. The True Christ is the Truth. One that's above and beyond and not native to any Religion...

For once you've elevated to your Christ level, you have risen high above the partisanship and trivialities of Religion. You have intrinsically become part of all the people, and are beholding only to Love.

The True Christ is you at your highest plateau; it's you at your absolute best: Which means at that point, you'll be overflowing with love".

The truth is, the world has never been without Christ's. There have always been and will forever be Christ figures walking amongst the people. No offense! But you will never find them quoting scripture in any of these oversized churches. The problem is; the sensationalism of Jesus has blinded us as to what a True Christ really looks like. At this precise moment I'm editing this chapter, a True Christ by the name of Nelson Mandela have successfully completed his journey and transitioned on to the spirit world.

Eternal Praises to the great Nelson Mandela!

I also view people like Martin Luther King Jr, Gandhi, Bob Marley, Harriet Tubman, Malcolm X, Mother Teresa and my grandmother Beryl Belfor as just a few of many of the Christ figures that have already transitioned on to the spirit world.

What I really want my readers to understand is that

it is intrinsically possible for us to become True Christ. The main purpose of this book is to provide the inspiration and enlightenment necessary for us to reach our highest plateau of righteousness. Hopefully leading to more of us elevating to the level of True Christ. You see the people that have long controlled us, never wanted us to know that it is possible for us to get to such an extraordinarily high and mystical level. They knew that if we did, they would lose all control. But I'll say it again, once our lives are consistently filled with love and we firmly embrace truth whenever and wherever we find it, all the toxic and debilitating grime and negativity we've been mired in is going to be stripped away. Allowing us to be free to fly and be as high and as good as we aspire to be...

In closing, I would like to bring attention to a glaring mistake that we humans have been consistently making. We always seem to put way too much faith in the messenger rather than the message.

"*When the message is true it is perfect, but the messenger does not have to be. So we must honor the message more than the messenger, and the message that will reign supreme and true for all eternity, is Love*".

Seventeen

The Spiritual Warrior

(The Liberator Of Love)

"*I*'ve climbed the highest mountain to bring this song: (For You)! Walked through the dreaded jungle to bring this song: (For You)! I've embraced the mighty warriors to bring this song: (For You)! To bring love and unity to this sacred land: (For you)"!

"I've fought the fiercest battles to bring this song: (For You)! Conquering the dreaded dragon to bring this song: (For You)! Chosen by the highest power to bring this song: (For You)! Bringing joy and happiness to this sacred land: (For You)"!

"I've endured endless pain, just to bring this song: (For You)! Seven years of suffering just to bring this song: (For You)! Walked through the burning fire to bring this song: (For You)! Bringing peace and harmony to this sacred land: (For You)"!

These are three verses of my song titled Te' Te'. It is a metaphorical depiction of the battles that's emblematic to the rise of the Spiritual Warrior; Similar to the metaphysical and physical battles men like Malcolm X, Bob Marley and Martin Luther King Jr must have had to endure, in order for them to have gotten to the level where they were able to inspire the changes that have brought good to humanity. (In the case of Nelson Mandela, it was more than 27 years of incarceration).

Out of the love for humanity the warrior is born. Out of the tireless search for truth, understanding and wisdom the warrior is born. Out of the darkness of bigotry and oppression the warrior is born. Out of the relentless battle to overcome both mental and physical adversity the warrior is born. Out of the sheer disdain for injustice and greed the warrior is born. Out of a burning desire to heal, enlighten and liberate the warrior is born. Out of the ability to overcome many trials and tribulations the warrior is born: Never bowing, and never giving up.

Spiritual Warriors are mystical forces, which at some point during their lifetime have had to have endured and overcome some form of adversity as part of their initiation and development. Hence why they possess such great power and vision. They often defy human logic. On a physical level, spiritual warriors regularly find themselves alone; but spiritually they are never alone. They are consistently connected to and surrounded by ancestral spirits of extreme and unimaginable power: An army of great spiritual warriors who had at one time (sometimes even more) walked the earth prior to transitioning on to the spiritual realm. These warriors are there for assistance and guidance.

The Spiritual Warrior exists in a world where coincidence is literally non-existent: A world of truth and balance where everyone and everything has a purpose. The Spiritual Warrior is both humble and aggressive. Contrary to popular belief, the Spiritual Warrior sometimes knows fear, but is never overcome by it. The Spiritual Warrior is a conqueror that sees light in a sea of darkness. The Spiritual Warrior possesses great love, and as we all know love conquerors all. **Therefore any battle that the Spiritual Warrior chooses to fight must always be just and righteous.** *The Spiritual Warrior is a winner that transforms hopelessness into glory. The Spiritual Warrior is both magical and realistic: Who not only has the gift of flight, but also the capability of invisibility. Meaning! Sometimes we can become invisible to our enemies in the midst of adversity, or any individual that might be obstructing our pathway. In other words like ghosts we will walk right by them without them seeing us. True!*

The Spiritual Warrior is a prophet and a healer who

is capable of healing with a simple touch, word or projection of energy. The Spiritual Warrior lives on the mountaintop and sees all that has to be seen. The Spiritual Warrior is a true angel of The Most High Creator whose generosity knows no bounds to those who truly deserve it. The Spiritual Warrior is a defender of Truth and Liberator of Love. So the question now is, who are you? Or better yet, who do you aspire to be? If your answer is the Spiritual Warrior, then by all means you should do all you can to become it...

So close your eyes in meditation so that you can feel and know the unbelievable power that abides within you: That which is the essence of who you are, your Inner God. Listen to the divine Wisdom and Truth that emanates from your Inner Voice and Love, Love, Love!

Eighteen

Sun of God

(Let The Sunshine In)

*Q*uestion! *Is there anything within our Galaxy that compares to the awesome power of our Sun? Is there? Well! Let me be honest! I really didn't need you to answer the question. I simply wanted to awaken your consciousness...*

Now that it's awakened! I'll be short and direct while putting this as nicely as I can without limitation or exaggeration. So here goes!

As humans our level of gullibility has been unbelievably deplorable. We have not only proven ourselves to be uncivilized, but our behavior can too often be described as being senseless and psychologically embarrassing.

For us to believe that the entity that created our

Universe and the man alleged to have been crucified on the cross 2000 years ago as being one in the same is ridiculous beyond words. To believe that God allowed himself or even his only son to be dragged through the streets, mercilessly beaten and crucified for any reason, is frighteningly insane. When it comes to religion, it is stunning to me how supposedly intelligent people (even some with PhDs), can prove themselves to be supremely unintelligent by throwing common sense completely out the window. This clearly shows how highly effective brainwashing can be. *Although there's absolutely no hard evidence or proof of his existence, we consistently give thanks and praise to the phantom of a man who is said to have been the only Son of God: That in all likelihood never truly existed. Yet we very rarely acknowledge or show enough appreciation for the awesome energy that we clearly know sustains all life on earth, the Sun. The True Sun of God that is.*

Listen! The most powerful energy in our Galaxy is the Sun. And though it is a staggering 93 million miles away from our planet, whenever it rises we can feel its awesome power. It's so hot and blindingly bright we can hardly get much closer to it without being burnt to smithereens. It is a much more impressive and truthful representation of our Creator's power than anyone who could have allowed themselves to be nailed to a cross by a gang of mere mortals. On the other hand, there's no way we can survive on earth without the existence of the Sun not even for a day, much less for 2000 years. When it's done, the Earth and everything on it is no more. There's no human who've ever lived that compares to this fiery power on any level. So the next time you decide to begin your day with a prayer or an affirmation, do me a favor! Turn to the east and pay some respect and homage to the power that truly sustains all life on this planet, **The Sun!**

So Hear Me!

"The time has come for Earth's children to awaken their consciousness and release their plaguing toxicities; holding nothing Sacred but the Truth...

The time has come for us to put all weapons aside and firmly embrace the spirits of Forgiveness and Fairness as we Atone for our Transgressions: Harmoniously coming together in Divine Unity under the Most Beautiful and Powerful Banner of Love...

The time has come for us to live in a world without borders, where there's no need for passports: Where Freedom and Peace flows freely like the river that flows unencumbered from the Mountain to the Seas".

Nineteen

The Road To Inner Peace

(Wow! He seems Happy)

*I*nner peace and happiness go hand in hand. For the most part they are both internal issues. You can't have true and lasting happiness without possessing inner peace; it is impossible. To encounter any individual that truly possesses inner peace is an extremely rare occasion. The closest most individuals will ever get to a state of inner peace is toward the end of their mortal existence, if at all. There are many who will simply pass on without ever knowing it. Then there are the unscrupulous ones who in my opinion will never know peace, neither in this lifetime or the afterlife. I guess that's what we would call Hell. Unfortunately, this chronic absence of inner peace is the norm for most people, and it really doesn't have to be.

The main purpose of this book is to take us higher towards that divine place where we all could find Inner Peace. But before we could get there, we first need to uncover the hindrances that have been blocking our paths. In other words we need to expose our demons. So what are our demons? Our demons are the toxic components of our society we have for too long been accepting and embracing. The more we embrace our demons is the more troubled and lost we will become. Thus making it impossible for us to ever get to a place of inner peace. At this point of the battle we are simply being destroyed by our demons; they're beating the crap out of us. They are winning! But the war isn't over yet; and I intend to finish it with our hands raised in victory... The purpose of this book is to expose and defeat our demons; once exposed, these demons become weaker and much easier to conquer. Once they are conquered, our pathways to inner peace will become much clearer.

At this stage of the book I have already identified most if not all of our major demons. Such as our religious beliefs just to name one. So there's no need for me to go over them at this point. We simply need to work towards overcoming them so we can continue on our journey towards making Inner Peace our normality.

But as we travel on up that road, there are some key essentials we must possess in order for a successfully journey to be assured. And in case you haven't noticed, I said up the road as opposed to down for a very specific reason. Inner Peace dwells at the mountaintop where Martin Luther King Jr stood before he transitioned on to the Afterlife. It represents the height of spiritual growth and consciousness. This is the only place where the Promised Land becomes a reality. This is the only place where we can clearly envision it.

*With that, let's talk about those key essentials. And there is no better way to start off the conversation than with **Truth**. Truth is extremely essential to inner peace and everything else. Without it there's no way we can attain inner peace. We should always seek out the truth and be ready, willing and able to give it full consideration in everything we do. As I've previously said, **"Any structure void of truth is destined to crumble. And whenever you compromise the truth it's simply not the truth anymore, which means** without truth **you're basically living in a fantasy world"**. You can never go wrong by embracing Truth. So let's seek it out with unwavering relentlessness and persistence and it will surely put us on the right path: The path to fulfillment and glory, or as I prefer to call it the glory road.*

*The other key essential is **Love.** It is the most important essential of not just inner peace but everything else. As I've consistently stated throughout this book, we simply cannot do without love. And* *though it seems like I'm being redundant, I have no choice but to repeat myself, it is what it is! You simply must have love in your heart and love for humanity in order to get to the mountaintop. Love also brings a whole lot of goodies with it such as compassion, kindness, forgiveness, patience, contentment, positivity, tolerance, the ability to trust, beauty, happiness and of course God just to name some.*

Love makes us warm and more attractive. It puts a consistent smile on our faces and gives us that beautiful glow. Love makes us healthy. It guarantees our salvation. Love is divine and selfless. I say this because many of us confuse our superficial and emotional obsessions with divine love. But even on that basic superficial level we need to be much more conscious of our actions. How can we truly love anything that we've been consistently locking up in a cage? That's not love; it's actually very cruel and selfish. And it applies to everything, particularly our mates, so be very careful. You simply cannot fall in love with a lion and then spend all your time and energy attempting to transform it into a pussycat if you know what I mean. "Before we can truly love anyone, we must first know, respect and accept who they truly are; and not our fantasized or unrealistic and sometimes insane version of who we want and expect them to be. We must allow them to fly or roar if that's what they were meant to do".

Getting to a level of inner peace is more about healing not just oneself, but also the world. Every time an individual gets to a level of inner peace it makes the world a whole lot better. Inner peace takes us to a place where we can be extremely rich without possessing material wealth. Where we are thankful and grateful for each and every day of life. It takes us to our highest plateau. So let's get there with Divine Love and Truth.

Twenty

The Afterlife

(See You Later Alligator)

*W*hat is the Afterlife? Does it really exist, or is death final? These questions have long been the subject of much contention for the history of humanity. Unfortunately we haven't had anyone physically come back to give us the full details of their long afterlife experience; at least no one I'm aware of. So my view on this topic (like most other topics) is going to be more of a spiritual one. Which in my opinion should actually be better seeing that the afterlife experience if it does exist (and I truly believe that it does), is likely to be more of a spiritual one also.

My belief is that our physical life span, is simply one of many crucial stages in the great pantheon of our continuously evolving spirit: A spirit that spans all eternity. Sooner or later we all have to make the transition from the physical realm into the spiritual realm and beyond! Which would obviously mean that *what we refer to as death is in no way final. It would only be the end of our physical existence and not the spiritual. From my prospective, our spirit adheres to a completely different set of rules and realities. My wisdom tells me that a bullet or a physical illness such as cancer can destroy the body, but it cannot destroy our spirit. So when the body dies the spirit simply moves on. Many people may say they believe in the concept of everlasting life, but in reality they're just not too sure. We seem to mainly believe only in what we can see with our naked eye. Which gives us a very minuscule, limited and often flawed account of all the things actually happening around us. This is why it is so vitally important that we learn to rely more on our consciousness, rather than our peripheral vision.*

As I stated earlier, our spiritual or third eye vision is far superior to our physical eyesight. But even on a physical level, there are some things we definitely know exist that we are completely unable to see with our naked eye. A perfect example of this is the oxygen we breathe. Without it the body eventually dies. And although we cannot see it we all know that it does exist. Well! The spirit basically works the same way. When it permanently leaves the body the body has no life. And although we haven't yet mastered the technology to clearly see it, it makes a lot more sense to assume that the spirit is alive and present even after the body is lifeless. So for us to believe that a person's spirit dies when they get shot through the heart, would be similar to believing that a bullet could somehow kill oxygen; Which to me, doesn't make good sense...

Based on some of my personal experiences of connecting spiritually to individuals who were several hundred miles away, I have no doubt that the spirit is a separate entity from the body. The way I see it, our spirit controls our body similar to how we control a vehicle when we drive it. So just as we are not limited to the confines of our vehicle, our spirit is not limited to the confines of our body. So the more conscious we become of our spirit, the more we will be able to connect to each other on a higher level spiritually even though we may be far apart. We may also be able to connect to spirits that have already transitioned on. Makes sense: I'll say so!

Now that we've gotten that out of the way, Let's talk about the quality of the Afterlife. I truly believe the quality of our afterlife experience will ultimately be determined solely by how well we behave in this lifetime. I clearly don't see Religion having anything to do with it whatsoever.

Contrary to popular belief, I don't view Heaven and Hell as being specific places. I see them more as quality descriptions of the afterlife experience. So let's say you've always been a greedy and dishonest person, regardless of your religion, your afterlife experience is

probably not going to be too pleasant, at least not materialistically. Likewise if you're an evil person, I'll say your afterlife experience is likely to be a very hellish one. In other words, the people who have lived their lives in a more loving, kind and generous way are more likely to have a beautiful afterlife experience. Hey! I don't know about you, but this theory makes a whole lot of sense to me.

If you really think about it, nothing really dies. Everything in existence transitions from its current form to either another form, another stage, another realm or maybe all the above in some instances. In my opinion, we either need to replace the word death with the word transition, or redefine it. To view death as final truly defies the laws of nature in my opinion.

Although I don't buy into the theory that we've evolved from apes, I do believe we are continuously evolving on a higher level.

Another thing I've noticed is that infants at the beginning stages of their life and adults nearing the end of their lives, both seem to have a heightened sense of spiritual consciousness. This leads me to believe there's some form of recycling going on with spirits that are newly entering the physical realm. Which buys into the theory of reincarnation.

At the end of the day, it's all about the spirit and the power it possesses. Whenever I think about the unimaginable vastness of our Universe, it seems to me the only thing in existence that possibly has enough speed and power to fully explore it is our spirit. My feeling is that our spirit handles time and space in a way, which enables it to go way beyond the physical capabilities of humanity.

The bottom line is! **If we truly believe The Most High Creator is good, then there's absolutely no way that physical death can be bad for those among us who have lived a righteous and loving life, regardless of religion. One thing I'm completely convinced of; is that death is definitely not the end. It's simply the beginning of a new existence, a new life! The AfterLife!**

Twenty-One

The New Beginning

(It's A Brand New Day)

*W*elcome to the Warrior's Realm. A realm of Peace, Freedom and Empowerment: A realm overflowing with a limitless abundance of knowledge, wisdom and understanding. A realm where truth has proudly reclaimed its true identity and love in all its glory majestically sits on its divine throne.

If you have gotten to this point, I trust that you have read this entire book. If so, I first want to applaud you and thank you for taking this spiritual journey with me. Whether you've realized it or not, you have just been handed the keys to the gateway of a new world, A New Beginning. A place where you're fully aware that your spirit is not only eternal and all knowing, but capable of flying faster than the speed of light: A place where you're finally able to overcome your social demons by shedding Religion and embracing Spirituality. A place *where you know the undeniable truth that Divine Love is the only pathway to your salvation; for once you're filled with Love you're filled with God...*

You're at a place where you don't worship the Christ: You become it. You're at a place where your God is truly your own...

The keys you currently hold in your hands are the keys to your Liberation. Now it's up to you to use them. If you do I can promise you, it will truly be The Start of A Brand New Day.

The Chosen

Here I stand before you, Resolute! With my feet firmly rooted to the ground and my crown emanating the brilliance of the Sun... My spirit soars with blinding speed through the Universe. My purpose is unshakeable and my vision clear... I am enlightened with the inspired truth of The Creator. My obedience to him has lifted and empowered me. It has made me right with righteousness and good with goodness. It has made me sure as sureness itself. It has filled me with the wisdom of the wisest and consumed me with love. I am purified!!! I am the hope of the hopeless, the innocent and the oppressed. Hate has forever been my enemy and I will forever be its conqueror. I carry with me the torch of healing and enlightenment. I stand here before you as the liberator of love, peace and truth, for I am The Chosen!

Black Warrior

The Closing Word

*W*isdom says! A truly rich man is a man happy and contented with the little that he has, not one who's mired in abundant materialism. Not one whose spirit is heavy with the excesses that he has been needlessly hoarding...

*W*isdom says! Wherever you find me you'll surely find Truth. And truth brings with it not only simplicity and clarity, but also Freedom...

*W*isdom says! Love will bring us Peace and Peace will bring us Happiness... Therefore isn't it better to have a small pamphlet that simplistically guides us to Peace, instead of a humungous maze of confusing contradiction???

Think about it!

www.ingramcontent.com/pod-product-compliance
Lightning Source LLC
LaVergne TN
LVHW011152080426
835508LV00007B/363